THE DURBAR

THE DURBAR

MORTIMER MENPES

GYAN

Published by

GYAN

Gyan Publishing House
5, Ansari Road
Daryaganj, New Delhi-110002
Phone: 011-47034999, 9811692060
E-mail: books@gyanbooks.com

Distribution Network
gyanbooks.com
India, USA, Canada, UK, Australia, France

ISBN : 978-81-212-9216-0 (PB)
First Published, 1903

2nd Impression 2023

Printed at: Gyan Press, Delhi.

THE DURBAR
Author: MORTIMER MENPES

THE DURBAR

LORD CURZON IN HIS STUDY AT DELHI

In the face of many obstacles and predictions of failure, he organised and carried to a triumphant issue the celebration of the accession to the British throne of King Edward the Seventh.

THE DURBAR

BY MORTIMER MENPES

TEXT BY DOROTHY MENPES

CONTENTS.

LIST OF ILLUSTRATIONS

I

THE S.S. *ARABIA*

A TAILOR

I

THE S.S. *ARABIA*

LIFE on board ship, with its flirtations and petty quarrels, is a familiar theme. Peninsular and Oriental journeys are very much alike. They are characterised by the same lazy life, the same bad weather, the same iced food, and the same deck sports. There is even about a P. and O. boat a certain familiar odour. Thus, a description of the journey from London to Marseilles in the S.S. *Arabia*, *en route* for the Delhi Durbar, would be rather tiresome.

The great excitement was when, early one morning, we arrived at Marseilles and leant over the rails to watch people embarking. They were distinguished folk and interesting. It was a fascinating scene, this gay French port, with its crowds of lace- and flower-vendors, the musicians with their guitars and mandolines, the acrobats, the carriages arriving, the passengers' luggage being hauled about, and the voluble French porters—all a-bustle to the sound of a dozen different tunes, which were being played by a dozen different musicians at one and the same moment. It almost reminded one of a scene from a Gaiety comic opera; and one expected every moment to see that clever comedian, Mr. Edmund Payne, appear on the scenes, in company with Miss Katie Seymour, to say that he was "tired of carrying the luggage from the station."

The first passenger to set her dainty foot on board the *Arabia* was Mrs. Craigie, looking radiant and charming in a coat of silver fur. Immediately in her wake came Lord Stanley, beaming and happy, his arms full of small bunches of fragrant violets. As he reached the middle of the gangway, a buoyant figure sprang along four steps at a time, almost overtaking him. This was Colonel Frankie Rhodes. There was no mistaking him. Who else so young, so energetic? He had almost reached the boat when he turned and saw Lord Stanley with his violets. Immediately he wanted to know where Stanley had found them; and on being told they had been bought from two or three stalls

LATE AFTERNOON

in the market-place, the gallant Colonel, anxious not to be outdone, fled back to the shore. We watched with interest his energetic figure threading its way among the different flower-girls, buying every bunch he saw. At last he darted forward—he had found a stall behind a pillar that Lord Stanley had overlooked—and a few minutes afterwards he came on board laden with violets, triumphant.

While this was going on, the passengers, with their luggage, had been arriving in streams—judges, peers, duchesses, proprietors of patent medicines, and celebrities of all kinds—one continual stream. In the midst of the arrival of Grosvenor Square, with its pomp and bustle and importance, I turned to watch a group of acrobats vainly trying to attract our attention. It was in December, early in the morning and bitterly cold; and to see these poor little people, in their torn pink tights and their gaudy waistcoats, with the spangles wearing off, vainly trying to be funny—this was pathetic. There were children, boys and girls, none of them older than ten, springing about on their fathers' shoulders, clapping their blue chapped hands, laughing and making jokes, yet never raising a smile. No one even noticed them, and the poor little ragged cap so eagerly stretched up to us for pennies almost invariably returned empty and unregarded.

The first meal after the arrival of Grosvenor Square, which was tea, was an interesting gathering. It reminded one of a Private View at the Royal Academy, and the questions and the remarks one heard on every side by the ignorant and curious were very amusing. "Now, who is that over there?" you would hear some one ask. "Oh, that is Mrs. Craigie!" "And that beautiful woman just behind her sipping her tea?" the interrogator would continue. "That is Lady Poynder." "Who are those men?" "That man over there with the happy face is Mr. Reed, the *Punch* artist. The other is a proprietor of a patent medicine, the greatest advertiser, they say, in the world; and that man in the check suit is Sir George Goldie, eminent empire-maker." And so on. What struck me most was the stateliness of the women. They were all tall and beautiful. I should think one might safely say that never before has so small a space held so many beautiful women as the saloon of the *Arabia*. The conversation, too, was sparkling. The newcomers had got over the fatigue of their train journey;

A BLAZE OF SUN

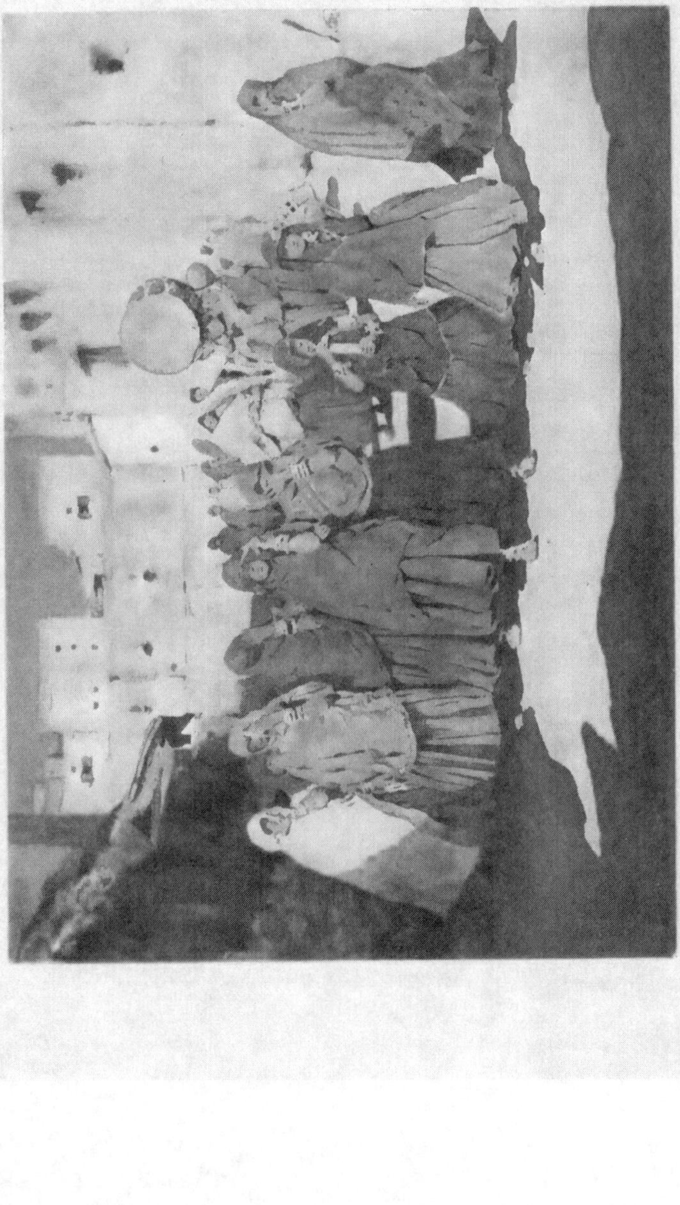

the boat was steady; and, what with the stimulant of the tea and the excitement, every one was intensely happy.

It was curious to watch the change which slowly but surely crept over the party towards dinner-time, when the ship began to roll a little —the sobering down, the dwindling of the conversation, the rugs and books that were brought out, and then the utter prostration and carelessness of appearances—all the usual symptoms of the malady of the sea! At the same time, I was struck with the courage and determination of Grosvenor Square. One could not help feeling a certain respect for the splendid way in which they fought against this sadness that was creeping over them. The night was promising to be extremely unpleasant. A plucky peer twice attacked his dinner, and twice had to beat a retreat. Certainly there was a marked contrast between tea and dinner. The joy and brilliance had evaporated.

The bad weather did not last long, and Grosvenor Square soon developed sea legs. There was very little incident. Each day was very much the same. Every one sat on deck. Here and there you would see groups of people playing bridge, a judge intent on a game of chess, an empire-maker talking about operas to a duchess, and the proprietor of patent medicine talking in the smoking-room of the difficulty the President of the United States would find in running things without his aid.

It was an ideal atmosphere for the artist: all were so considerate and sympathetic, so intelligent, so strong in artistic instincts. They would come up and ask you how your work was going on, and if they could do anything for you; and altogether they were extremely helpful. A long line of people went down to the saloon every day to be sketched by Mr. Reed. He began very gently with only two or three sitters; but gradually the line became longer and longer, until there was a great stream of subjects every morning, like sheep being led to the slaughter. You would see Reed come up on deck, spot a man, go up to him, and lead him away by the arm—first a judge, and then a duke, and afterwards a soldier—and all would go down, with quick, nervous steps, trying to look unconscious, and as though they had been in the habit of being sketched daily. They evidently did not dislike it—in fact, I think they rather enjoyed it—but they were shy. It was the fashion every afternoon for this sketch-book

A RETAINER FROM RAJGARH

to be passed round for general inspection, and it was curious to see the amused, tolerant look on the faces of the people change into a sickly smile as they came across their own portraits. One waited regularly for the subjects of yesterday to come up to you and say, "Well, what do you think of Mr. Reed's sketches? I think that the one of the Duchess of Marlborough is good, and some of the men are excellent; but that one of me, you know—well, there is no character in it —no one would recognise it. Yes: I must say he really seems to have failed over me." The drawing of a very plain gentleman was so good that the aim of every one on board was to keep it away from his beautiful young wife.

There was one lady who occupied a great deal of attention. She was interesting from the moment we left Marseilles until we dropped anchor at Bombay. She was a very old lady, and always dressed in black—a soiled black dress and a black bonnet which was never quite straight on her head. From the first she was thoroughly pleased with the Peninsular and Oriental line of steamers. She went up to the stewardess, and detained that good person for over half an hour to explain how pleased she was with her cabin.

Then she attacked the head steward. "I am thoroughly pleased," she said, "with my seat at table. This is a very nice boat, and I am greatly attached to every one on board." She always wore the same black dress and the same black bonnet by night and by day. Her luggage consisted absolutely and entirely of kodak films. She informed every one that she was treating the Durbar purely on artistic lines, and that she intended photographing Lord Curzon and incidents by the way. This old lady was a source of great interest. No one talked to her willingly, for that involved hours of conversation. We had all tried, and, as the saying goes, "once bitten twice shy." The officers were the most long-suffering, and any one of them would sooner swarm up the mast than encounter "the woman in black." A clear circle was described about her wherever she went. Still, she was always alert, ready to buttonhole some ignorant and innocent passenger; you could not catch her napping. She photographed every one and everything. On a dark rainy day, when it was utterly hopeless to take a photograph on deck, the old lady would walk boldly into the saloon, and take a picture of the entire boat at tea. She would come up to you and snap her

AWAY FROM THE SHOW

kodak four inches off your face, and then look away and think how subtle she had been. I have seen her, as we were nearing a port, rush below to get her kodak, and on the way up, catching sight of herself in the mirror, eagerly photograph it. Then she would come up on deck, and, quite forgetting what she had intended, would run her camera right into Lord Stanley's broad back as he was looking at Aden, and take a snapshot—Ping! Lord Stanley was her favourite subject. She used to photograph him in every attitude—at dinner, asleep on a deck chair with his mouth open—anywhere, everywhere. When any one questioned her, she said that she was the wife of an eminent professor, and that she was going to Delhi to take a photograph of Lord Curzon. And there she was on the 1st of January, in the same black dress and in the same black bonnet, photographing the Viceroy!

Of course, there was the inevitable American girl on board. She appeared towards the end of the pleasant voyage: at least, it was only then that we discovered her. She came at a moment when all had said all that they had to say to one another. She flashed like a meteor into our midst, and then, meteor-like, disappeared. She was a typical American girl, beautifully dressed, and knew to a nicety how to put on her clothes. She had a pronounced Southern accent; but she took the boat by storm. We called her the "Gibson Girl." One day a gallant colonel was chatting to a clever artist. C. A. said to G. C., "There goes a beautiful woman!" G. C., who had great habits of ladies' society, said, "I quite agree with you," and bravely set out without a word to storm the citadel. Within five minutes he was in the midst of an earnest conversation which lasted for four days, and for four days we saw nothing more of the colonel. He was occupied. That started interest in the Gibson Girl; but the other men were less bold than the colonel. They used to come in swarms, and beg him to introduce them, bribing him by choice cigars and all other conceivable means. It was useless. The colonel was obdurate, and refused to introduce to her a living soul. It was only on the day before we arrived at Bombay that there was a general introduction to her; and that was at a dance, when the colonel was powerless.

A well-known conjuror, an old gentleman, came on at Aden. We all clustered round him on deck. Every one on the boat was there, and every one was

A RETAINER OF THE MAHARAJA OF CUTCH

enchanted. He made chickens come out of eggs and fruit trees grow up from seeds. He gave us all nicknames. The Duke of Marlborough was "Mr. Smith." "Now, Mr. Smith, I want you to give me your ring." The Duke did not feel inclined to give his ring, and refused. "Well," said the conjuror, turning to Lord Stanley, "Mr. Masher, you can give me your ring"; and Lord Stanley, who is the soul of good-nature, instantly gave it up. We were all interested in watching the conjuror, and I heard some one just behind me say in a very rapid tone of voice, "How dexterous that was—simply marvellous!" I turned round. It was the Grand Duke of Hesse. He was enjoying the conjuring just as a child would. He took a coin out of his pocket, and showed me how one of the tricks was done. He used a great deal of action, and spoke in rapid English with a slight accent. He executed the trick far more cleverly than the conjuror.

One morning early the Duke called me up to look at a sunrise. I found him on deck, worried and perplexed. "What does this mean?" he said. "Surely Nature is not herself this morning? She is doing something very quaint." Indeed, she was. The sea was of a dull leaden colour; the sky was brilliant mustard-yellow; and in the midst of it the sun was rising, a vivid lemon-green, just like an unripe lemon. Certainly I had never before seen such a combination of colour, and I admitted that Nature was indeed behaving strangely. The Duke of Hesse is himself an artist, a man of great appreciation. He was very interesting when he talked of the Queen—the "Great Queen," as he called her, Victoria. He said how absurd it was to say that the Great Queen never painted from Nature and that many of her works were touched up by her masters. He told me that many a time when he was a little boy he had accompanied Her Majesty on sketching expeditions, that he might hold a glass of water for her as she painted. Often he had to rush off to the nearest stream to change the water, and be back in double quick time lest she should lose the fleeting effect of a sunset. There was no doubt about it: Queen Victoria always painted from Nature; and it was extraordinary, the Duke told me, how true her sketches were in general effect. Then he talked of the Queen's capacity for work. State documents were always smothered with marginal notes in her own handwriting.

A STREET SCENE

Her Majesty's knowledge of State affairs was quite marvellous. She possessed great powers of persuasion, and sometimes influenced people merely by being persistent. The Duke when a boy often heard long conversations between Queen Victoria and her Ministers. If they refused to give way to her views, she would be so persistent and hold on to her own opinions so tenaciously that in the end they gave way. In foreign politics she was a real power. She had great knowledge and influenced her Ministers to an extraordinary extent. No one but her own family ever knew how hard Queen Victoria worked. Sometimes he would see a light burning in her study window at two or three o'clock in the morning; and on slipping up for a few last words before going to bed he would find her in the midst of many papers, working as hard as any newspaper editor.

The Duke of Hesse is a very clever "contortionist." He can do any mortal thing with his limbs. One day, when we had retired to a quiet corner of the deck, where the Duke was to show me how he could bring the sole of his foot right up to his face, an æsthetic lady appeared on the scene, and said, "Ah! I suppose, now, you two are admiring that sunset together?" and we had not the heart to contradict her. The Duke is enthusiastic and energetic. He gesticulates a great deal in ordinary conversation, and, in order to keep his legs from swinging about with his arms, he is compelled to sit upon these members, Chinese-fashion. He is a splendid athlete and very strongly built. One curious thing about him is that the two sides of his face are quite different one from the other. If you look at him, profile on one side, you think that he is one man; and if you look at him, profile on the other, you take him for some one else. He is just like a boy—young, fresh, possessed of tremendous vigour and the temperament of an artist. There was a bet as to the distance of the boat from the land. He was anxious to find out the Captain's opinion, and, without thinking, flew up the steps leading to the bridge. When he got to the top he caught sight of the Captain, who is rather a martinet; and flew down again quicker than he came, eight steps at a time. He was loved by every one on board, and was utterly simple, getting joy out of everything. I noticed him spend half an hour one day watching the antics of a cat just as a child would.

A DISTINGUISHED NATIVE REGIMENT

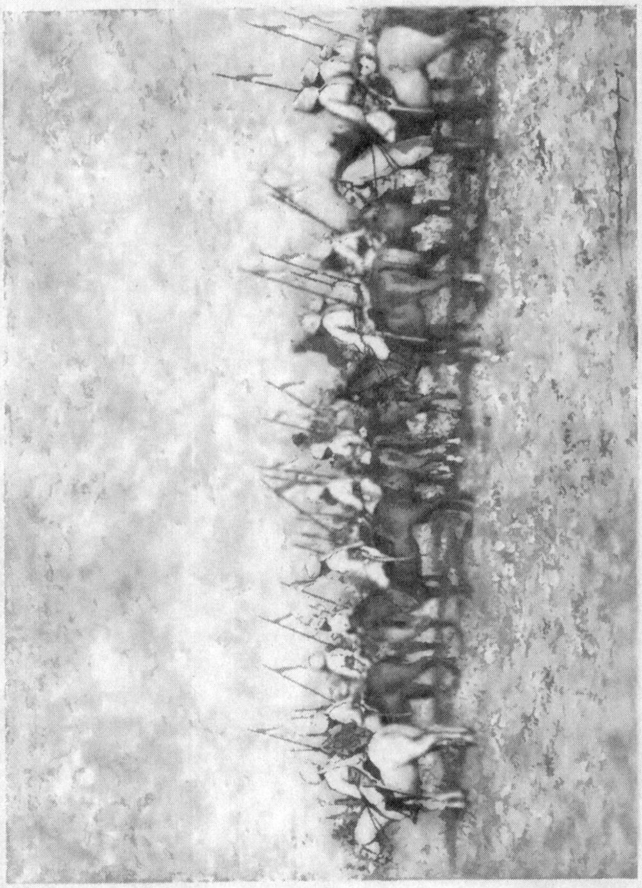

II

SETTLING INTO CAMP

II

SETTLING INTO CAMP

We took the ordinary train from Bombay, and started long after the "special" containing the Viceroy's guests and Lord Kitchener's. At a station half-way on our journey we came across Colonel Rhodes and Lord Stanley drifting about the platform and looking solitary. They had just left their train in a siding, they said, and were waiting until the mail train passed by. This was at night, midnight, and it was bitterly cold; but all the special-train people were trying to prove what a splendid time they were having, and what a delightful life it was in India. Still, they seemed worried at being left in a siding. As our train steamed past them we saw Colonel Rhodes and Lord Stanley playing a game of bridge.

When we arrived at Delhi we had to collect

our luggage, a feat that required enormous energy and dexterity. It was perhaps one of the most interesting scenes ever witnessed at a railway station, and we lingered a while to watch it. The English valets were paralysed in the confusion. Their masters had to attend to everything. There were officers wheeling trucks, free fights, ladies wringing their hands over lost boxes and quarrelling over the possession of trunks. I was surprised at the very unusual violence of the officers. They kicked the men about them, and swore appallingly. I saw one man tear a trunk away from a railway official, wheel it off, and then spill the contents. It was perhaps the most confused mass you could possibly imagine—such a medley of different nationalities! There among them was our thin black servant, a man who was of a higher caste than the rest, slipping in and out of the people and gathering our luggage without any trouble at all. He was our salvation, and he seemed in an extraordinary way to command respect. Nearly every one else was desperate. The stationmaster gave up shouting orders which were not heard among the confusion of tongues, and stood still, merely whispering. The man into whose shoes he had stepped, I learned, had gone mad

SCENE OUTSIDE THE RAILWAY STATION DURING THE DELHI DURBAR

Always a remarkable sight, and thronged with people at all times of the day.

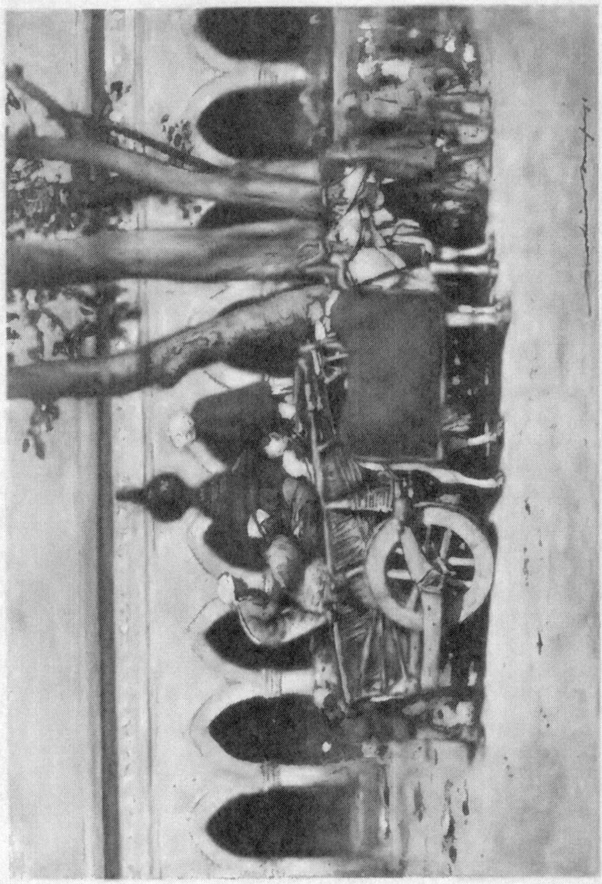

before the arrival of Lord Curzon's guests. Now that they had come, this one was dazed. The strain was too much for him, and he collapsed.

When we arrived at Number One Camp we found that it was a camp for millionaires only. In fact, it was commonly called the Millionaires' Camp. Everything was terribly expensive. One cannot but admit that things were wonderfully well managed. We were shown to our tents, and found that there was very little to complain of. Then we went to interview the officer in charge. We found this poor gentleman literally besieged. The tent was surrounded by masses of men and women. We elbowed through to the inner circle, and even then had to wait some time before we could so much as see the officer. Most of these people were asking the young man futile questions. Just as we entered we heard a lady talking in a very high voice. She demanded of the officer what he proposed doing for the poor cattle. "It is a crying shame," she said. "All the way down from Bombay to Delhi I saw from the carriage window cattle so thin that their bones stuck out of their flesh. It is a sin that you can do nothing to remedy it." The officer was for the moment at a loss how to answer her; but he had tact, and he explained kindly that it was the nature of the animal for his bones so to protrude. There were crowds of people all asking similarly absurd questions. One woman wanted to know if he had found her muff. She had been driving about the different camps (scores of miles) all day, and had dropped it somewhere—where exactly she did not know—but she wanted it found. The officer answered her courteously. "Really, madam," he said, "I think, for a serious matter of that kind, you had better go and see Colonel Baring." I heard him directing nearly every one to the Military Secretary, Colonel Baring. One man, a knight, elbowed his way into the crowd waving a telegram over his head, and shouting to the officer in stentorian tones: "What do you propose to do for us? We have only single tents. There are no drawers or cupboards or any accommodation for clothes. My wife's and my daughter's dresses cannot be hung up, and there are fifteen cases of them. And here is a telegram which, if something is not done immediately, shall be sent off to one of the morning papers." He read aloud the following message:—"Arrangements in Number One Camp broken down. Guests leaving Delhi." The poor officer merely shook his head, and said,

ON DURBAR DAY

VETERANS sitting in the sun before the Durbar.

"I think, sir, you had better see Colonel Baring." It was amusing to see how all these people with their complaints were despatched to the Military Secretary. All that day there was a clump of agitated people not only overflowing the tent of the officer in charge, but also streaming fifty yards around, and always a thin line of them oozing out on their way to the Military Secretary. I myself wanted to know something; but, finding it almost impossible to push my way through, I started off independently to visit Colonel Baring. We hailed a tonga and went off to this demigod; but on the way we thought better of it, and decided to start with the Viceroy's camp. We found our way to the tents of some friends; but at the various doorways we were always met by native servants who canted their heads in the palms of their hands, and said, "Sick, sick." It was obvious to us that our friends were all sick. Then we went to the Commander-in-Chief's camp, to call on Colonel Rhodes, knowing him to have been in hale and robust health when we left him at the station some hours previously. Here too we were met with canting of the head and the same "Sick, sick." Things seemed to be becoming serious. It was obvious that some terrible epidemic had seized upon the Viceroy's guests. We saw as we passed the great man Colonel Baring surrounded by a block of people and well-nigh inaccessible. Therefore we called on the Viceroy's private secretary, Sir Walter Lawrence, who had promised to help us in every way. We found him in his tent in the midst of work, and told him of the trouble in the Commander-in-Chief's camp. Every one seemed sick and ill, we said. He was quite composed. He had not heard of it. When I described the pantomime with the servant, the head in the palm of the hand, he said, with a smile, "Oh dear no! That was *sleep*, not *sick*. I don't think you will find sickness in this camp." Neither I did. All seemed very healthy and wide-awake. Colonel Baring was not at all the sort of man I supposed him to be. Directly he saw me he said, "What can I do for you?" It was said so crisply that I felt he could do nothing: there was nothing I wanted him to do. "Tell me," he said, "is there anything I can do? Have you places to see the Durbar?" I said I had. "Then," he said, "do you want special facilities?" I jumped at that, and said that I did; and he wrote me a letter saying that it was the Viceroy's wish that I should be helped in every way. And that letter proved to

A HORSE FROM JODHPUR

An animal whose antics, as he passed the Viceregal daïs, aroused the utmost enthusiasm.

be of untold service to me. It was a key which unlocked every barrier. In the end this wonderful man satisfied everybody. It was amazing how crisply and quickly he arranged everything. Every one in the end was impressed with Colonel Baring's tact.

The Durbar was wonderfully organised. To think that this big city, as large as Greater London, was a few short months ago nothing but rice-fields! Now it was illuminated by electric light; there were tramcars; it was an enormous town, and one that looked as though it had always been there.

Camp life in India is not like camp life anywhere else. It is reduced to a state of perfection. It affords the greatest possible comfort. I for one could never find anything to complain of. We visited Number Two Camp towards the end of the Durbar, and the people there were just squaring up their accounts. They found that they had been paying enormous sums for their meals. That was nothing compared with the "extras." They had been in the habit of having an extra little square of cake with their tea every day, and at the end they were charged two rupees for each piece of cake; and the last breakfast in camp, which consisted of bread and butter and eggs, cost them eighteen rupees. Here and there one met with complaints of that sort; but on the whole the arrangements were satisfactory, and every one was delighted. The postal and police systems were not all that one might have wished for. We marvelled sometimes how letters ever reached their destinations at all. The native postmen would come up to you in the streets at all times of the day, and without saying a word would thrust a letter in your face to see if it belonged to you. There were scoundrels about the camp as servants who called themselves Bombay boys; but, through the kindness of the P. and O. superintendent at Bombay, we possessed a genuine Bombay boy, and he was a treasure. He could do everything—dress hair, fold clothes, pack, and be valet as well as lady's-maid. There were very few Bombay boys. The bulk of servants were men who had crowded into Delhi in the hope of being employed, asking double and treble their proper salary. The life we led was different from that of most of the people at the Durbar. Most of them spent their time in one whirl of gaiety—luncheons, dinners, teas, receptions. There were things going on all the time. People were simply gorged with gaiety. There was too much

CAMELRY FROM ALWAR

They carry the ancient swivel-guns—brightly polished metal guns—which shine so brightly that one can see them from a great distance.

of it. What we did was simply to rise at daybreak, paint in the early morning, and go back to breakfast. The getting of the breakfast used to be rather difficult. There were very few servants, and they were men of different nationalities. Some of them were Chinese. One had to order things by pantomime, and sometimes it was quite three-quarters of an hour before we could get what we wanted. We always wrote an order for a carriage, and what time it was to call, the day before. All the tonga and carriage business at the camp was wonderfully well arranged. After breakfast we usually went to the camp of one of the native chiefs or to some big ceremony. In the afternoon there were always polo and football matches; but while these things were going on, we were always painting in the streets or in the native camps.

At the end of the Durbar it was extraordinary to see the worn-out aspect of the people who were presumably enjoying the holiday. They had seen too much; they were tired; it must have been a relief to them when it was all over. We in the Press Camp enjoyed every minute, and, as we one and all said afterwards, we should like to have had the whole fortnight of ceremonials over again. The presence of so many beautiful English women did much towards making the Durbar a success.

Of course, there were very many dinners to attend, and it was marvellous how well all the Viceregal parties were arranged. The night I dined with the Viceroy there were over a hundred guests. One enormous tent was used as a dining-room, and another equally large as a reception room. Every one agreed that Lord Curzon was an ideal host, and the memory of the A.D.C.s was wonderful. They knew the names of every one there. My personal experience was not especially enlivening. I sat near a lady who scarcely spoke a word during the whole evening. Once she turned round, and said, in a gushing manner, "Isn't this an interesting dinner? Do you know, we are all distinguished and interesting people here!" I could not but take her word for it. It is impossible to contradict a lady.

STATE ENTRY

As seen from the Jumma Masjid.

III

THE STATE ENTRY

ON THE STEPS OF THE JUMMA MASJID

TENS of thousands listening for a signal—the Royal Salute—to say that the Viceroy had entered the Imperial city.

III

THE STATE ENTRY

On the day when the Viceroy was to make his state entry into Delhi we were up at dawn, shivering with cold but enthusiastic, and anxious to be off, for we knew that our tickets, though they would admit us to the Jumma Masjid, did not reserve seats there. Our tonga was yellow—a brilliant lemon-yellow—drawn by a white horse whose bones stuck out pathetically, and driven by an aristocratic old gentleman with a beard dyed magenta to hide the ravages of time. He was a person of some importance and some caste, as one gathered from the contempt with which he treated the world: from the stately policemen down to the naked water-carriers, all classes were the same to him, and he struck at their faces indiscriminately as they came into our path. It would not have done for the Park, this lemon-yellow tonga; but there was a great fitness about it. It was a capable vehicle and very healthy.

I shall never forget the traffic on the way to the Jumma Masjid, a confusion never dreamt of in Piccadilly; even a Derby-Day mob would pale beside this crowd of native sightseers. Myriads of carriages passed and repassed, all going in different directions. There seemed to be no definite arrangement. The police were doing their work exceedingly well; but a regiment of soldiers would have been powerless in such a throng. It was simply one mass, spreading over the road and overflowing on to the pathways and into the ditches—one seething mass. Carriages and foot-passengers were jumbled together in inextricable confusion; the screaming, the jostling, the noise, was beyond description. Never within the memory of man has such an extraordinary collection of vehicles been gathered together. There were tongas of every conceivable shape and form: some gaudily decorated and filled with gaily-dressed natives; others, plain and khaki-coloured, occupied by dust-begrimed Europeans; antiquated broughams and victorias drawn by every kind of animal from a mule to an elephant; crack cavalry regiments, their accoutrements glistening in the

A NATIVE BULLOCK-CART FROM BIKANIR

THIS is a marriage-cart. The silver cloth of mail on the bullock is as fine in workmanship as that on a lady's chain purse.

morning sun; racing camels passing rapidly by with their long, shambling gait; shabby landaus filled with gorgeous native gentlemen and followed by their retainers; coaches occupied by young English misses in muslin frocks, men in uniform, and smart society belles—each and all on their way to the Jumma Masjid. The dust embraced and enveloped us, Europeans and natives alike; dust lay thick on our carriage cushions; dust entered at eyes, nose, and mouth, and choked our utterance. Slowly the great stream of traffic moved on—a swaying, screaming, jostling, noisy mass.

How we reached our destination is a mystery to me. One little incident enlivened the tedium of the journey. There was a fight between two elephants. Bored and irritated by the long wait, one elephant made a dash at another, and a battle ensued. Ere long, from somewhere in the background, another elephant appeared upon the scene —whether instigated by his keeper or not I cannot say. On he came, lumbering along, his trunk swinging, a sagacious look in his eye, determination in every step. Right into the middle of the combat he marched, looked down on both his brethren somewhat scornfully, and then began to hammer and belabour the biggest, the bully.

With a calm judicial air, beautiful to behold, he chivied the unfortunate animal about until it was thoroughly cowed and dispirited. Then as majestically as he had come he sailed away, his devoir accomplished.

I was greatly struck, as we moved slowly along, by the kindliness and gentleness of the natives. In this dense mass of handsome dignified people one felt curiously sordid and stupid and out of place. This Durbar, with all its gorgeous pageantry and native magnificence, seemed no show for the Saxon. Its mere existence had been brought about for the glorification of our most powerful and splendid race; yet wherever one saw a European in Delhi his presence jarred upon you. You felt that he was a blot in an otherwise harmonious whole. We are strong physically as a nation, and it was marvellous to watch how an Englishman jostled his way through the crowd and forced himself in front of the natives; but it was not a pretty spectacle. In the midst of a sea of gorgeous colour, a rainbow crowd of slim, graceful figures, with all the dignity of the East in their bearing, this elbowing wedge-shaped form, looking almost like a torpedo in its attitude of violent determination, gave one a pang. As he

A RETAINER FROM JIND

pushed and cuffed the men about him one felt a sensation of shame.

On the way we passed a long line of retinue elephants, belonging to the ruling chiefs, waiting to join in the procession. They burst on our jaded senses and dust-dimmed eyes like a dream of the Arabian Nights suddenly come to life. It was a foretaste of what was to come. We knew now that our eager expectations were not to be disappointed. The Durbar would be more than we had anticipated. This was a splendid rehearsal of the great ceremony that I was to paint, and a splendid opportunity to study these gorgeous creatures quietly; but I was foolishly reckless. I was like a greedy boy with a plate full of strawberries, trying to cram them all into his mouth at once. I feasted my eyes on each elephant; I gloated over each magnificent combination and each harmony, the emerald greens, the carmines, the violets, the golds, and the vermilions; and the result was that, before I had passed more than half the glittering throng, my sense of colour was exhausted. I was satiated: I had seen too much. Then I realised that here in India, to avoid the danger of becoming colour-blind, one should nurse one's eyes, not stare and exhaust oneself in colour, but always keep some strength in reserve.

Major Dunlop Smith was in charge of the saluting elephants. "This is an anxious moment for you," I cried, as our tonga drew up for a moment before his white charger. "Good heavens, man," he answered, "it will be the happiest moment of my life when I see the last of these brutes! At any minute there may be a grand burst-up of the whole thing. One slip, one fractious elephant, and the procession is thrown out of gear! Any moment this may happen. I daren't think of it." I myself thought, as I saw him manage his cumbersome troop, that under his vigilant eyes there was little fear of calamity.

I shall never forget my first sight of the Jumma Masjid. It was worth coming from the ends of the earth to see. What was it like? What can I compare it with? Anything that we in England have ever seen? I think not. Perhaps a garden is nearest to it—not a Surrey garden planted with stocks and mignonette, but an ideal garden such as we have all dreamed of, with banks studded with gorgeous, flaming tropical flowers. No: that will not do: it must be a garden of jewels, a garden set with jewels, with pearls,

AKALIS FANATICAL DEVOTEE

ONE of the aged Sikh warriors who fought so bravely for us during the siege of Delhi.

sapphires, rubies, and diamonds. How impossible this scene is to paint—impossible to imagine, impossible to describe! The streets, the houses, the roofs, the steps, and the benches massed about the Jumma Masjid teemed and vibrated with colour; the flower-beds stretched far as eye could see; it was a garden for a fairy princess. Poor painters, poor palettes! How futile your efforts must be!

We felt like beetles, dull-coloured beetles, and terribly Saxon as we forced our way among these living flower-beds and mounted up to the terrace reserved for Lord Curzon's guests. The temple was already filled with people, a brilliant throng, the women in their gayest dress, and all the men in uniform. I discovered the vantage position for painting, and flew to it, only to find a little ticket pinned to the seat with the name of a well-known artist on it. After wandering round for some time in search of a seat, at last I found a very good position for my work. One man rushed up to me and said, "Menpes, rejoice! I have saved a wonderful place for you in the tower—simply superb!" "Yes; but I have already got two lots of seats," I explained. "Never mind. You shall have three. You shall rush about from place to place. I guarantee that yours will be the best pictures of the state entry." With that this energetic little man hurried me off to the tower. I saw that this position would be of no earthly use for my purpose: it was too much of a bird's-eye view. In fact, the whole building seemed wrongly constructed from the painter's standpoint. It was too high up. I began to wish that I could have a position on the steps of the Jumma Masjid among the Moslemin, so as to be more on a level with the procession as it passed. I asked a young A.D.C. if this were possible. He answered immediately in the affirmative with the alertness and intelligence which characterised all Lord Curzon's staff of helpers. He introduced me to an old native official in a gorgeous costume, a man of some position and well known to the populace. This gentleman, he explained, would take me into the crowd and clear a space for me wherever I chose to paint. Looking down upon the surging mass of people packed as closely as mosaic, I thought it impossible that there could be a square inch of space among them; but directly the gold-laced aide-de-camp appeared above the steps and the gorgeously-dressed official followed by myself descended, the mass melted and separated, leaving a long, clear pathway.

A FAMOUS LED HORSE IN THE RETINUE OF THE RAO OF CUTCH

No one but a Maharaja or the son of a Maharaja has ever ridden this noble horse.

It was a kindly, gentle crowd. No one came near me, no one even touched me: perhaps because from their standpoint I was too mean a thing to touch. No one stared at me: perhaps because I was not sufficiently decorative to arouse their interest. Certainly I felt rather a poor creature standing in the midst of these stately people. All this preparation—the pathway cleared, the gold-laced aide-de-camp, the gorgeous official,—what was it for? I took out my paint-box and blushed. The folly of it, the absolute futility! Here was I standing before a scene which no artist save Turner should ever have attempted to paint, calmly unfolding a stupid little paint-box and squeezing out tubes of Reeves's water-colour, pigment which, compared with the glowing tones around me, looked like mud. Still, I shut my teeth firmly and went on doggedly, scarce knowing what I was doing, but trying to brazen it out: I too am an Anglo-Saxon. Presently I plucked up courage; for there, a few yards off, was another of my craft working away with pencil and note-book. This was energetic little Melton Prior. He also was out in the crowd, but rather more to the fore than I, and right on the line of route.

As I worked, my vigorous friend of the tower

episode forced his way through the crowd and stood at my elbow. He stood there for some minutes without saying a word. I glanced down at him. His face was purple; his breath came in short gasps; he seemed ready to burst with some hidden anger. Too much occupied with my work to care what happened to any one or anything, I laconically inquired what was the matter. Then he broke forth. He had been turned out of the tower. I had been turned out of the tower. Six members of Parliament had been turned out of the tower. All this was to make room for Lord Curzon's friends. The legislators had been allowed to remain there for two hours only: to be turned out at the last moment neck and crop without a word of warning! I murmured something about the tower not being such a good position, after all, as I squeezed out some more rose madder. "Yes; but you don't understand," he spluttered excitedly. "The position is not especially good; but I am slighted, you are slighted, we are all slighted." At last I turned round, exasperated. "My dear fellow," I said, "I don't care a brass farthing whether I'm slighted or not! All I want is to paint this picture. Now, just look for a minute at the gray of that sky. Would you believe that——"

SHAN CHIEF AT THE DURBAR

ALTHOUGH never having visited India before, these chiefs watched the gorgeous retinues of the Indian princes pass by with perfect equanimity.

He was gone. I was talking to empty space. Disgusted with my lack of sensitiveness, he had turned on his heel and marched off to air his grievances elsewhere.

Later in the day I met the very A.D.C. who had caused all this disturbance. "You've distinguished yourself now!" I cried. "Oh, I know they are all awfully cross. It had to be done, you know. I couldn't help it," said he.

All these minor disturbances affected me but little. Did the fate of nations lie in the turning out of the members of Parliament, I should, I am afraid, have been but little perturbed. There were several hours to wait; but, with so much to study, time could not pass otherwise than pleasantly. It was a blaze of colour—simply a blaze! To see the artists with their boxes vainly trying to paint was pathetic. I looked at my poor little palette of colour and dragged myself about the place limply. Rembrandt couldn't have painted that scene in black-and-white. He might have suggested it, but only to one who had seen it. Then one felt the value of precious stones to work with, or something very different from ordinary pigment. It must be painted in the jewel-like, gem-like manner, and bit by bit, facet by facet. To attempt to paint it in flowing water-colour were to reproduce a sunset in silhouette. The crowd was a mosaic one, and the people were like living tapestry. There were lilacs, violets, grass-greens, apple-greens, lemon-yellows, oranges, and little splashes of jewel-like colour formed by the turbans. The background to all these wonderful tones was gray, a sombre gray monotone. Delhi is not a red city brilliant and full of colour. It is a gray city. The sky, though blue, was a sad blue. The streets, the buildings, the earth, the dust, all were gray. What setting could be more exquisite for the jewels before me, what background more perfect for the pictures that were to come, the gorgeous pageantry that was to sweep over this lovely colourless canvas?

As the time drew on one began to feel nervous and restless. The tension was too great. We couldn't talk. We could scarcely think. We simply held our breath, and waited. The crowd of natives remained passive. Nothing seemed to affect them. They showed no emotion, made no demonstration, throughout all the long hours of waiting. You couldn't tell what they were thinking about. They were just a dignified crowd. You felt that this was not their show—that it roused no enthusiasm in them. Some of their

AN AKALIS FANATICAL DEVOTEE

This old warrior is such a religious enthusiast that on the day on which the birthday of Govind Sinh was celebrated he clothed his pony in a pair of drawers and thus made a Sikh of him, for this article of clothing is one of the five things essential to the true Sikh.

own smaller processions would have interested them infinitely more.

Of course, as the cannons boomed forth the royal salute, and one knew that the procession was well on its way, the inevitable animal appeared on the line of route, the wretched mongrel Derby dog. The dramatic moment was spoiled; the magic silence was broken; thousands of eyes were riveted on the creature; dismay and annoyance fell upon the heated and harassed officials. Full of occupation, gay and careless, quite oblivious to viceroys and processions, the Derby dog whirled and circled in the dust. Impudence was his characteristic. He would threaten an elephant or bite a Maharaja with equal indifference. Wherever there is a procession, a review, a Lord Mayor's Show, he is always there. He will even attend a funeral, and wait until the burial service is being read to bark at the bishop. Forbid all dogs, chain them up, expel them off the face of the earth, and he would still be there—this sandy-coloured, tousled, short-legged, mongrel dog. Still, he served his purpose here in India. We were all so unnerved and strained that it was untold relief to laugh even at a puppy.

Every spectator amongst all those thousands

felt the impressiveness of the moment. Every eye was strained for the first sight of the glittering throng. Every one was waiting for the first notes of the National Anthem. Slowly the blazing procession came into view, unwinding itself and presenting a wholly new scheme of colour every moment. It was never the same. It was as hopeless to follow each effect in detail as to catch every flash in the swimming skirts of Miss Loie Fuller. Each instant produced its own glory.

I shall not attempt to describe that scene as I saw it. I have neither the power nor the presumption for such a herculean task. It would only end in failure, in a dry catalogue of an artist's colourman. All I can do is to mention roughly the various sections as they passed. First came the Dragoon Guards and the Horse Artillery; then the heralds, picturesque figures, with their silver trumpets and mediæval dress; the Viceroy's bodyguard on fine bay walers; and the Cadet Corps, handsome slim young figures in their gorgeous blue-and-white uniforms, headed by the dashing Sir Pratap Singh. It was the elephants we had come so many thousands of miles to see; and we held our breath until they appeared, swaying and irresistible—a gleaming, glittering,

LORD AND LADY CURZON ENTERING DELHI

This elephant was used by Lord Lytton at the previous Durbar.

bejewelled throng. One felt a thrill of patriotism as a magnificent elephant towering high above all the rest came into view, the handsomest and finest of all, at sight of which thousands of voices as though from one throat murmured, "The Viceroy!"

Every hat was raised, every turbaned head bent low, before that youthful, joyous figure under the glittering golden umbrella. One felt that no other Englishman could have carried himself better or have fitted into that magnificent picture more perfectly than Lord Curzon. He was the right man in the right place. His elephant, you felt, was an animal created for regal processions, for carrying the representatives of kings—slow, massive, majestic. The huge beast seemed conscious of his success. He was also conscious when he was being made a fool of. There were two clowns in the procession, the pantaloons, the jesters in a solemn scene. One carried a chandelier on each tusk, and another sheepishly fanned the flies off his master with a huge feather punkha. They hated it, these elephants, just as much as a schoolboy when he is made to kiss a girl in public; but to us they were a relief from so much dignity, and acted as an antidote, as did the Derby dog.

How shall I describe that retinue of elephants?

I tear my hair, and think, and think, until I feel I must go mad. I see it all so clearly: can I not coin words? Can I not dip my pen in purple and gold? It was almost like looking at the sun. Yellow spots danced in front of one's eyes: one had to turn away into the gray courtyard, and lose an elephant or two, to get relief. You could not see the procession in a continuous way as a whole, because of the blinding colour; but by treating it almost scientifically, by nursing oneself to see colour intelligently, one obtained swift, true impressions of crisp, luminous pictures that burned deep into one's brain. Most people gazed, and gazed, and were blinded, exhausted: they lost all feeling for colour.

This was a scene for Turner. Turner, who could paint the sun, was the only man to paint this procession of native rulers. You never seemed to get the last word in colour. An elephant would pass covered with cloth of gold and ropes of pearls. "This is the finest of all," you would say; "colour has gone as far as it can go." Then suddenly another marvellous combination would spring upon you: a group of elephants in gold, emerald green, and jewels, looking like bubbles ready to burst with brilliance, and making the surrounding colours faded

BURMESE ELEPHANTS AT THE STATE ENTRY

THESE elephants in order to reach Delhi in time for the Durbar started from Burma in October, walking several thousands of miles.

and pale by comparison. For once one felt grateful to the dust, the dust that at times rose in clouds and hid portions of those marvellous colour-schemes from our sight, as with a curtain of yellow gauze, bestowing upon them a dream-like mystery marvellously enhancing their unearthly beauty. Every now and then an elephant would rise clear and tangible from this dream of Arabian Nights, and one would catch for a moment a glimpse of some historic potentate, only to be lost the next moment as he passed into the throng of his fellows.

For hours that seemed unending the great procession dragged its glittering pageantry along. The different races gathered together from the length and breadth of India were singularly impressive. Fierce, white-robed Baluch and Pathan chiefs who had never even seen one another before, riding side by side with European officers—what a contrast! There was the sullen Hyderabad, with his beautiful note of yellow, and Lord Kitchener riding alone in his uniform of a General, his hand resting on his side,—not the stern, impassive figure we read of in newspaper reports, but ruddy-faced and happy, the smile on his lips broadening to a beam as he passed the Jumma Masjid, where many of his friends were assembled. As the end of the procession passed I rushed back to the Jumma Masjid, and, gazing far ahead, watched this great pageant like a spangled serpent glimmering through zones of light and shadow into the opalescent distance, scumbled with the eternal dust.

The day was over. Every one was exhausted, limp; everything about us seemed squalid and sad. Only then we remembered that we were starving. Colour for the moment is all-satisfying; but the effect wears off. The next thing to do was to go home. Getting back to camp was always a serious part of the day's work. For hours we wandered about, vainly trying to find our little lemon-yellow tonga. Luckily, we came across a learned professor with a group of friends who had travelled with us on the *Arabia.* We sat down on stones and held counsel. The professor said we must treat the situation from a purely military point of view: it must be thought out systematically. A body of scouts was formed, and I was given a very prominent position. We started with very clear ideas as to the carrying out of this manœuvre. We had brought it down to so fine a point that to miss the tonga was a sheer impossibility. Had it not been thought out scientifically and proved by algebra?

A ROYAL RETAINER OF RAJGARH

Suddenly a shout indicated the tonga had been found. And—oh what humiliation!—by the doctor, who had scoffed at our nicely-laid plans and trudged off pigheadedly on his own account! We crowded round him excitedly. "How did you find it?" "What system did you work upon?" he was asked. He had no imagination, and his explanation was crude in the extreme. "Well," he said, "there's nothing much to tell. I was walking along, and I ran into the tonga. I knew it belonged to Menpes, because it was yellow." Because it was yellow, forsooth! It hurt one's sensitive feelings even to hear him. With pained expressions, we got into the tonga and drove back to Number One, the camp of the millionaires, not at all a fitting place for a painter, its very atmosphere spelling philistine materialism. At luncheon there was the usual struggle on the part of every one to describe what had been seen during the day, and the conversation was richly flavoured with such comprehensive adjectives as "sparkling," "gorgeous," "magnificent." How much meaning do such descriptions convey to those who did not witness the pageant?

IV

THE PROCLAMATION

A JAIPUR HORSEMAN

He carries the silver trident of Jaipur.

IV

THE PROCLAMATION

THE great day arrived, the day on which His Excellency Lord Curzon proclaimed at Delhi the Coronation of His Most Gracious Majesty the King, Emperor of India. Although the ceremony had been postponed for half an hour because of the new moon, which obliged the Mussulman chiefs to worship at the Jumma Masjid, by ten o'clock the roads were thick with traffic of all kinds—silver and golden carriages carrying the chiefs and their attendants in gold-embroidered coats and turbans weighted with precious stones; smartly-equipped landaus and victorias containing British officers, civil and military, smothered with orders; judges; generals; governors and consuls; distinguished foreign visitors; representatives from Europe and the far West, Japan, Siam, Afghanistan, Burma, Baluchistan, and almost every part of the world; men on camels; natives in tightly-packed wooden carts; regiments of cavalry, British and native. It was one continuous stream. As we circled out of Number One Camp in our little yellow tonga, we worked our way into this long procession and formed part of the slowly-moving stream of humanity. It was impossible to see where it ended and where it began: all one could do was to travel slowly onward. Now and then an adventurous man would dash ahead by digressing into a ditch, almost capsizing in the attempt; but for the most part the procession never varied, and the same vehicle kept in front of us all the way to the amphitheatre.

It was an impressive sight as we approached: the great brown, far-reaching plain, and the white and blue horseshoe-shaped amphitheatre, with its arcaded galleries and tiers of seats, its cupolas gleaming in the sun, and beyond, the huge army of the King Emperor, 30,000 men, horse, foot, and artillery—one broad sweep of bristling forces. The long procession of carriages was packed with wonderful order and precision. Each person was given a number identical with that of the driver. Twelve thousand people alighted, gradually filing into the amphitheatre as they took their places.

A PATHAN HORSEMAN

These men are celebrated for their magnificent horsemanship.

The organisation was perfect. We brought a servant with us to carry our luncheon, and he joined us there, but had forgotten the lunch. Through the courtesy of Mr. Barnes, we held four tickets and a permission to wander about the amphitheatre and sketch during the ceremony. We left our seats in charge of the servant, and moved in the arena with the crowd. The sights we saw—the groups of natives and the chiefs and princes in their gorgeous costumes—were almost beyond description. I should think that never within so small an arena have so many precious stones been massed together. You could scarcely look anywhere without seeing a blazing jewel. All the most notable men in India were assembled in that amphitheatre. There were the Nizam, in a plain, dark blue uniform with a yellow turban; the Gaekwar of Baroda, in white satin; and hosts whose names we did not know. Perhaps those who attracted most attention were the Shan chiefs. They were wearing solid gold dresses, belling out like pagoda roofs, and great headgears of blazing gold. The crowd stared at them, and countless cameras snapped under their very noses; yet they never moved. We walked round the arena for about two hours; but whenever we returned there they were, still in the same position. One was standing with his arm on a chair; the other was sitting sedately. As they wore skirts, it was difficult to say whether they were men or women. They had never been to India before, or seen anything approaching this grand ceremony; yet they showed not the least emotion, staring stolidly before them like two of their own Burmese idols. The amphitheatre was a blaze of colour, nearly every man wearing a uniform of some kind. All the glory and pride of India were assembled—Pathans, Shans, Rajput chieftains, Baluchi chiefs. Gathered together under the roof of that great amphitheatre were representatives of one-fifth of the whole human race. There were emissaries from the old Powers of Europe too, the young Republic of America, and the great countries of the Far East such as China and Japan—tourists, soldiers, civilians, and, best of all, the beautiful Englishwomen. These outshone the glittering gorgeousness of the native princes by the sheer loveliness of their faces. The natives stared, the rajahs gasped, at sight of that bouquet of Englishwomen. It was superb. I am sure the world has seen nothing like it before, and I could weep to think that it may never look upon the like again.

A RAJPUT OF RAJGARH

It was a surprise even to India. All these natives must have gone back to their States saturated with pride and loyalty: they will never forget what they saw that day.

Towards the daïs the colour effect was somewhat spoilt. We were looking full at the sun, and could see nothing but a blinding white sky, while the crowds appeared misty and hazy. When walking round the arena quite close to the different groups the colour was quite gorgeous. From the artistic point of view, the only fault one could find with regard to the arrangement of the Durbar ceremony was the quality of red that had been used round the arena. It was of a bluish tint, and rather a mistake. At eleven o'clock a bugle was sounded, the arena was rapidly cleared, and all returned to their places. Two thousand men were massed in the arena playing stirring tunes to beguile the period of waiting. Every one had arrived. The amphitheatre looked one solid mass of people: in front the daïs, with its gold-embroidered carpet and silver chairs of State, and all round in the front row the long line of ruling chiefs—a blaze of colour. Behind the daïs was a gallery enclosed with latticed framework, in which the native ladies sat to watch the ceremony. There was a tremendous excitement when the Imperial Cadet Corps, with their blue-and-silver uniforms and jet-black horses, passed by—as fine a set of men as you could find anywhere,—all native rulers or the sons of rulers, trained as soldiers.

All eyes were fixed on a shuffling, shambling band of white-haired old men who came immediately after them, some of them on the verge of the grave, led along by stalwart young soldiers, and bravely trying to step out to the tune of "See, the Conquering Hero comes!" A thrill ran round the audience as they approached; for these were the Mutiny veterans of Delhi and Lucknow, the men who held India for the Empire on the Ridge at Delhi through heat and battle and pestilence and hardships. What a contrast!—these smart young cadets, and this rickety collection of old gentlemen, some in weatherbeaten tunics stained and faded with the sun, others in frock-coats of ancient pattern buttoned up the wrong way, but on every coat a medal! And the people! They stood up and cheered and shouted until they were hoarse; women wept hysterically, and strong men sobbed. The whole assemblage rose to do them honour. One felt that but for these men there would have been no brilliant pageant to-day, no

VETERANS OF THE MUTINY ON THE GREAT DAY

The most interesting incident of the whole Durbar was when these ancient soldiers marched into the arena to the tune of "See, the Conquering Hero comes!" Some of them were almost dying, but they stepped out bravely to the stirring old march. The entire audience rose to their feet, and cheer after cheer rent the air; for they all felt that but for these hoary, badly-dressed old men there would have been no Delhi Durbar at all that day.

Delhi Durbar. Age had laid a heavy hand upon the Mutiny heroes; but many of them marched with a firm, elastic step to the strains of the stirring old military march. One man, over a hundred years old and quite blind, was led into the arena by a young brother-in-arms; he turned his sightless eyes towards the cheering and feebly saluted. He dragged himself round the arena; but it was his last walk. He died the next day. The veterans took their seats amid tumultuous cheering. Some of them during the ceremony stole from their places and sat out in the sun. They were then in exactly the place where they should not be, and the native police gently led them away; but they crawled back, refused to move, and were left there. It was their day, and they knew it, and were allowed to do whatever they liked, even if it interfered with the march-past. Perhaps in all that splendid fortnight nothing made a deeper or more lasting impression upon one than the sight of these splendid warriors.

At noon we heard the skirl of the bagpipes, and a company of Gordon Highlanders, headed by pipes and fifes and drums, marched briskly into the arena with fixed bayonets. All of them were picked men, stalwart fellows who had seen active service. They were the Viceroy's guard-of-honour, and lined up smartly in front of the daïs. It was a hot day, and these men were standing with the sun full on their faces. They were all of fine physique; but the sun was too much even for them, and one by one of them dropped during the ceremony, and were carried away into the shade, until there were many gaps in the long, straight line.

Perhaps never before have so many cameras been at work together. Nearly every one had a kodak, even many of the natives themselves; and there was the sound of ping! ping! ping! all over the place, and the buzz of the cinematograph.

Suddenly we heard a rattle of muskets in the distance. It was the guns outside on the plain firing a royal salute—one long, continuous rattle, beginning very loud and going off faintly into the extreme distance. Each battalion took up the salute, one after the other; and the clean, sweeping way in which it was done was magnificent. Then a squadron of British cavalry appeared in the distance. It was escorting the carriage containing the Duke and Duchess of Connaught. As the cavalcade approached, we discovered that it was the Ninth Lancers—pennons fluttering and lances

A MOUNTED MACE-BEARER

gleaming—a magnificent regiment. They were greeted with cheers and shouts of "Bravo, the Ninth!" The Duke and Duchess received an enthusiastic welcome. The National Anthem was played by the massed bands, and the whole audience remained standing.

Their Royal Highnesses then took their seats on the daïs. The Duke of Connaught, who was in the uniform of a Field Marshal, looked a kingly figure sittting there, his gold baton on his thigh and his breast smothered with orders.

There was a pause of a few moments, and a dense cloud of dust was seen far off. It was the Viceroy. Gradually the Fourth Dragoon Guards came into view; then a flash of scarlet, the Viceroy's bodyguard; and lastly, the Imperial Cadets, resplendent in blue and silver. The Viceregal carriage was drawn by four magnificent horses with outriders in scarlet and gold. As their Excellencies ascended the daïs, the entire audience rose in their seats, a royal salute boomed out, the Viceregal standard was unfurled, and the massed bands once more played the National Anthem. Very beautiful in a pale blue dress embroidered with gold, Lady Curzon took her seat near Her Royal Highness. The Viceroy bowed to the

Duchess of Connaught and the audience, and took his seat on a marvellous throne upholstered in red velvet and ornamented with a golden crown and silver lotus leaves.

The picture was complete. It was the most brilliant assemblage one could possibly imagine.

Now all was ready. Sir Hugh Barnes stepped up to the daïs with a profound bow, and asked formal permission for the Durbar to be opened. The Viceroy assented; and the pursuivants, making deep obeisance, faced the arena and gave a signal to the bandmaster. Instantly the drums rolled, the bugles sounded, and the massed bands gave out stirring music. In answer there was a flourish of trumpets, clear, sweet, silvery notes; and the Herald appeared on his jet-black charger, a gigantic and stately figure, looking as though he had stepped from out an ancient page of British history. The sun shone upon the golden embroidery of his dress and on his silver mace. Following him came the drummer and twelve trumpeters—six British and six native, —in crimson coats ornamented with gold, the trumpets bearing the Royal arms and the Royal cipher embroidered on satin. They halted for a moment, and sounded another flourish. Then

A BEGGAR

they divided into two sections, joining once more as they reached the daïs. Again the trumpets sounded sharp and clear like a call to arms. The Herald saluted. Leaning forward, the Viceroy commanded him to read the King Emperor's Proclamation declaring the Coronation of His Majesty the King Emperor of India.

Absolute silence reigned throughout the entire audience as the Herald wheeled his charger round and read in a magnificently clear and resonant voice, perhaps the finest the world has ever heard, His Majesty's Proclamation. At the close he wheeled his horse round once more and saluted the Viceroy. Another flourish of trumpets was sounded, and the Royal Standard was unfurled, floating proudly out upon the breeze. The soldiers presented arms; the massed bands struck up the first grand notes of the National Anthem; and the crowd rose to their feet as one man, while a thrill of loyal enthusiasm ran like quicksilver round the arena. Then there was a pause.

That was the supreme moment of the ceremony. One felt it. It was dignified, impressive, and quiet, almost saddening, because it was so impressive. There was no frivolous talking, no cheering. It was simply a dead quiet. The sun shone upon the silver throne on the Viceregal daïs, on the glittering jewels in the amphitheatre, on the uniforms of the men; but, above all, it seemed to illuminate and linger round the central figure of the Viceroy, quietly clad in his official costume, standing in the presence of all those great oriental chieftains, upholding the supremacy of the Imperial raj. Never for one moment did he allow the quiet stateliness and the dignity of the Englishman to be overshadowed by the colourful magnificence of the oriental potentates. Nothing impressed one more amid the pomp and magnificence of this oriental ceremonial than the modesty of the Englishman who stood there bathed in the glory of the Eastern sun, holding in his hands the guiding strings of the British rule.

Then the guns on the plains fired an Imperial salute. There was another flourish of trumpets, and, rising from his throne, Lord Curzon addressed the Durbar. He spoke in a clear, calm voice, never faltering. The King's message to the Princes and People of India was received with loud cheers. So, also, was His Majesty's reference to the prospective visit of the Prince and Princess of Wales. The manner in which the Viceroy seized hold of interesting points of British policy, and

A RETAINER FROM CUTCH

placed them unflinchingly and vividly before his hearers, was exceedingly diplomatic. How he vindicated in their presence that rule against which their fathers had attempted to fling themselves five-and-forty years before! Thus were the martyrdoms of John Nicholson and Henry Lawrence proudly and for all time avenged. In the very place where the heat of the Mutiny had been greatest, all factions and all jealousies were stilled for ever. As he stood erect and strong, his left foot resting on a footstool, Lord Curzon looked a born ruler of men, a worthy representative of that Sovereign in whose name he wields a unique power.

His speech was greeted by a vast acclaim. Then the Herald and the trumpeters trotted into the arena, and lined up in front of the daïs. One silvery peal rang out on the quiet air; and the Herald, turning towards the audience, raised himself in his stirrups, waved his helmet on high, and shouted in his clear, reverberating voice, "Three cheers for the King Emperor!" In an instant the whole audience sprang to its feet and gave three mighty cheers for the first Emperor of India. The cheering was taken up by the troops on the plain outside. Their voices might have resounded as far as the gates of Delhi. They were almost loud enough to wake the buried heroes, and tell them that they had not died in vain.

Once more the National Anthem was played by the massed bands, and the pursuivants trotted out of the arena.

Then came the ceremony of presenting the ruling chiefs to the Viceroy and the Duke of Connaught. Sir Hugh Barnes stepped forward to ask permission, and one by one they filed past to do homage to the representatives and brother of the King Emperor. It was interesting to note the different bearings of the chiefs. Some, who had been to Europe, strode on to the arena in an assured way, shaking hands with the Viceroy and the Duke of Connaught, and backing out gracefully; others were shy and self-conscious; some lost their heads, and forgot the little speech they had prepared; some presented their swords; others merely bowed. Each chief seemed to vie with his neighbour in making a dazzling display of jewels. Every sword was encrusted with diamonds and rubies; every mantle was sewn with designs in pearls and precious stones. There were priceless diamonds of perfect purity on cloth of gold—one glittering line of treasure and beauty. It was interesting to witness the contrast of the

A SWIVEL-GUN BEARER FROM RAJPUTANA

various races. One and all lost their shyness when they reached the Duke of Connaught. He took them kindly by the hand, and said a few courteous words to each. Every man left the daïs with a contented countenance. First came the ruler of Deccan, His Highness the Nizam of Haiderabad, a loyal prince noticeable for his extreme simplicity of dress. He was followed by the great Mahratta prince, the Gaekwar of Baroda, in a white dress with a red turban and most magnificent jewels. His is one of the richest states in India. Then came His Highness the Raja of Mysore, a man with very large dominions; the Maharaja of Kashmir; the Rajput princes; the Hindu princes; the Mahratta chiefs; the Sikhs; the Indian Mussulmans; a striking figure, Her Highness the Begum of Bhopal, who laid a jewelled casket at the feet of Lord Curzon; Pathan chiefs; Shans from Burma; and chiefs from the Shan states. To mention each one individually would be impossible. One chief wore starched accordion-pleated skirts of brilliant green. A ripple of laughter ran round the arena as he appeared, and I heard one of the soldiers along the route say, "Hallo! there goes Fanny!" On the whole, however, the spectacle was most impressive.

At the conclusion of the ceremony of presentation Sir Hugh Barnes stood before the throne and requested leave to close the Durbar.

The Viceroy and Lady Curzon then left the amphitheatre. The Duke of Connaught followed. They were cheered to the echo. The vast crowd slowly dispersed. We all felt that we had been privileged to witness a great event destined to become historical for ever.

LORD CURZON AND THE DUCHESS OF
CONNAUGHT ON THEIR WAY TO
THE RETAINERS' SHOW

V

THE PROCESSION OF RETAINERS

A TYPICAL GROUP IN THE RETAINERS' PROCESSION

V

THE PROCESSION OF RETAINERS

OURS was a gentle start. We wandered about on the plain outside the arena sketching different groups, and had our breath taken away before the review began by pictures that were simply magnificent. One broad sweep of changing, glittering colour was stretched out before us for mile upon mile, formed of clumps of retainers from the tribes of India. There were tribes from Cashmere, from the highlands and the lowlands, camels, elephants, men in armour, animals in armour, and costumes of every conceivable colour and form. It was a bewildering show. Almost the first figure we saw as we approached was a man on horseback with a banner, a faded salmon-coloured banner, with a gold device on it, suspended from a long pole of carmine,—a splendid figure, powerful and full of dignity. His dress was of vermilion covered with chain armour, the vermilion breaking through here and there. On his head was a gold covering; his gray beard was combed from his chin upwards, and swept away on either side. The horse was almost as magnificent as the rider: it had cobalt-blue reins, vermilion and emerald-green checked saddle-cloth, with old-rose tassels, and a blaze of silver and gold everywhere. This creature stood just like a statue. He never moved. There he was in the brilliant sun, a picture waiting for me. I made a sketch of him.

To describe the scene as a whole would be impossible. All one can do is to give little peeps of the different groups we saw about the grounds. Suddenly we would run right into a gold-and-silver cart, a blaze of colour, a harmony in red, gold, and old-rose. The cart was of gold plush fringed with green-gold, and bearing a wealth of old-rose tassels. The oxen were draped with great coverings of blazing silver metal formed by myriads of small polished discs; their horns were encased in silver and tipped with gold; and round their necks hung strings of silver bells. The driver was dressed in clear brilliant blue touched with silver and a green-gold cap. Inside sat a figure

THE SHAN CHIEFS' RETAINERS AT THE NATIVE REVIEW

Major Dunlop Smith made them open their umbrellas at the last moment; certainly it added interest and brilliancy to the group.

clad in fair pink silk. Troops of camels passed us with emerald-green saddle-cloths, ridden by men in bright vermilion. The Baroda gold-and-silver cannons glistened like patches of living fire in the sunshine, and away above everything else towered an enormous erection with dozens of people inside. As we drew nearer we discovered that this was an elephant four-in-hand from Rewa.

Thus the motley throng went on, each group more dazzling and more barbaric than the last. It was an ideal opportunity for the painter. One does not more than once in a lifetime get a chance of seeing thousands of tribes together. Here we saw groups that we should never see again. Here were people, living thousands of miles apart, who had probably never seen one another before, camped so closely that one could move from State to State in a few strides.

Major Dunlop Smith helped us in every way possible. He was a conspicuous figure among this mediæval host. He seemed to be everywhere! One saw him on his white arab going from group to group encouraging and stimulating with his kindly smile and smoothing away difficulties as if by magic. He never missed a detail, and it was obvious to the most casual observer that this retainers' show was all Major Dunlop Smith from beginning to end. But, although in the midst of elaborate organisation, he always found time to dash up and point out a picture or describe a group of warriors. "How do you manage to know them all?" I asked him once. "Well, you see," he said, "I was afraid that these fellows would imagine they had been brought here to form part of a circus show; and if I can address them by their names, and say, 'Now, So-and-So, I am very much pleased with the way you have behaved so far: do your best in the arena,'—it helps things." Time passed all too quickly among this gorgeous assemblage, and before we were aware of it the Viceregal party had been sighted.

We stole back to our places just as the carriage swung into the arena. Lord and Lady Curzon, the Duke and Duchess of Connaught, and the Grand Duke of Hesse took their seats on the daïs. The signal was given: a wail of weird native music was heard in the distance, and the first of the brilliant pageant, a huge elephant hung with emerald-green and surrounded by mahuts clothed in crimson, loomed into sight. For two whole hours this moving band of colour circled round the

A STANDARD-BEARER

This is the State standard of Jaipur.

arena. State after State passed by, each one more bizarre and picturesque than the last. There were monstrous elephants hung with jewels; flaming banners; mail-clad horsemen; crimson velvet and cloth of gold; masses of precious metal; glittering fringes and tassels. It was almost too brilliant, too bright, too strange. One's brain could not take it all in. If you could only have arrested the procession now and then and isolated a portion of it, there would have been some chance of remembering and realising what you saw. That was impossible, and artists and writers groaned aloud with dismay as each new and brilliant combination of colour appeared. How could any one hope to convey any idea of that bewildering spectacle to the people at home? There are occasions when words are useless, and this was one of them. All the poor writer can do is to shut himself up and hammer away at it, sentence by sentence, picking and choosing his words, writing and rewriting.

It was quite an informal affair. The Durbar was more deeply impressive and the State Entry more significant; but both these scenes might have been repeated more or less exactly in London or elsewhere. The review of the Princes' retainers was unique. No one in that arena had ever seen, or ever would see again, anything to approach it. For days we had been satiated with marvellous spectacles and colour-schemes that left us breathless; but this was something different, something more wonderful than all. One felt that one was living in another world, the picturesque old world of a hundred years ago. Even Anglo-Indians more or less accustomed to such scenes could not but admit that here were types and costumes that they had never seen or dreamt of. It was not merely a Barnum's show to amuse the jaded Westerner: there was nothing grotesque or ludicrous in this array of native retainers. It was a historic pageant. Here were real men dressed in real costumes that they had lived in and knew how to wear. They carried with them their own atmosphere round the arena. Sometimes the different States followed so closely on one another's heels that their atmospheres overlapped; but they never intermingled—each one was isolated, separate, distinct. Nor was their arrangement the result of accident. Infinite care and pains had been taken in the massing together of the different States, and every detail of colouring or accoutrements was correct. For example, Cutch

EMBLEM-BEARERS OF CUTCH

One of these golden vessels contains water from the Ganges, and whenever the Maharaja is athirst he is enabled to drink of the water of the sacred river.

was a State that gave splendid scope for picturesque effect. This had been copied from two fine old original paintings of the Dassava ceremony held a century ago. Major Dunlop Smith showed to me the pictures.

We sat among the Punjaub chiefs to watch the procession. Young Patiala was just in front of us, and a gorgeous person in salmon and gold sat next. I didn't know who he was, and I did not dare display my ignorance by asking; but he was a very affable gentleman, and undertook of his own accord to describe the different States as they passed. "Look!" he cried, as a surge of red, violet, and glittering gold came into sight. "Here comes Cutch." I could well understand his enthusiasm as the groups drew nearer. Cutch was almost all gold—solid burnished gold. There were great blazing triangular-shaped fans of cloth of gold with colour breaking through them, sometimes salmon, sometimes emerald-green, and sometimes peacock-blue. Men on camels dressed in vermilion turbans carried salmon-and-gold banners surmounted by golden emblems. These banners and emblems played an important part all through the procession, and added their quota of colour and brilliance. They had been presented by the Mogul

Emperors, our friend in salmon informed us, and acted as a stimulus to remind the various States that they formed part of the Mogul Empire. Our friend of the green and vermilion checked saddle-cloth had an important position in this Cutch group, and as he sailed past us he blew out his whiskers with a self-conscious air. He seemed to have had an extra brush-up, and he looked so glossy that I almost wished I had waited until now to sketch him. Roars of laughter shook the audience as some men on rainbow-coloured stilts, their heads on a level with the roof of the arena, passed by. These stilted gentlemen, although they appeared somewhat ridiculous, were of the greatest possible service in actual warfare. Behind each man came a servant with a long red pole. For a brief moment I was confused; then I quickly realised that, of course, the pole was for support. A man twenty feet up in the air on stilts without any chance of rest is in a more or less hopeless condition, and this was simply a resting-pole. These warriors are very bold and brave people: they sometimes have to attack men on elephants and are carefully chosen for the task.

There was a pause, and a sound of quaint music reached our ears; as it drew nearer one realised

THE GOLD AND SILVER CANNONS OF BARODA

THESE cannons are of solid gold and silver. They are so brilliant that in the full sun of mid-day one can scarcely bear to look at them.

that there was a band of Arabs, and one could not help feeling as one saw them that at some distant period there must have been some connection between Africa and this portion of the coast. They were low-class people, these musicians, a sort of camp-followers and hangers-on. Only the very lowest classes in India can be induced to form part of a band. A Sikh never will. He is a fighter, and to walk about and play a musical instrument would be absolutely impossible. You could as easily picture Kitchener playing the concertina as a Sikh blowing a trombone: the thing is preposterous. Fancy Kitchener playing at a picnic—not all the time, but just when his special part came in!

Next came the gold and silver cannons of the Gaekwar of Baroda. As they advanced with the sun full on them, one could see nothing but golden rays shooting out from a clump of fire. Here was no tinsel, no Alhambra and Empire make-believes, but solid gold and silver. Even the horns of the oxen were encased in gold, and precious golden tissue covered the sacred beasts.

In the rear of Baroda came Gwalior leading Central India. Here one noticed a change. A levelling influence had been at work. The colour was a little saddening; and the costume was evidently disappearing, scumbled over by Western ugliness. The men knit themselves together and marched squarely in rigid lines. They were more angular and had less of that delightful swing and looseness so characteristic of the East. This group made one reflect, and it brought home to one the discouraging fact that the native costume is fast disappearing and giving place to military uniform. You could not help feeling that this Retainers' show would be the very last of the sort that would occur.

Our friend of the salmon robe showed the keenest interest in a group of bards that passed by, chanting as they went songs on the glories of their land. These men, he told us, are privileged people. All kinds of advantages are attached to their position. They may even go the length of informing the Chief of his shortcomings. True, they clothe their chidings in an artistic form. They have some little home truths to tell him, and they chant them in the form of songs in such a poetical way that half their sting is lost. In fact, it is a scientific study with these bards to wrap up bitter pills in the sweetest of sugar-plums. Stiff with golden embroidery, the Gwalior elephants

NATIVE BARDS FROM THE CUTCH STATE

Whose chief feature is a curious kind of bugle which at intervals gives out a curious kind of gurgling sound, much like a turkey in pain.

attracted all eyes. There were twelve of them—the first three of blazing gold, and the rest grading off to silver and copper, becoming paler and paler until they reached a neutral gray.

It was odd to see amongst all this gorgeousness a woman's covered litter pass; and I asked the salmon gentleman why it was there, and what it could be. He said that this was from the State of Bhopal, the only State in India ruled by a woman; and then began to talk to me about this woman ruler. It appears that wherever she goes the preparations for screening her from the vulgar gaze are most elaborate. If she attends an evening party a space is always cleared round about her; and a native never dreams of passing the Zenana save in a crouched position. Her husband has no social standing at all: he is almost like the drone in the bee-hive: even the sons are of more consequence than he. The daughter, curiously enough, occupies the same secondary position that a girl would in any native State: she is never mentioned. My informant was a most intelligent man, and as the procession passed I asked him questions about the wives of some of the native rulers. He told me how strict the etiquette was, and how careful one has to be in talking to men of their women-folk. For example, one could never dream of asking a Mogul if his wife were better when she had been ill: that would be considered too intimate, too personal. You should say, "I hope things are getting better in your house?" To mention the word *wife* is considered coarse and vulgar in the extreme.

This procession was more or less familiar to us. We had had it all paraded before us in miniature every morning for the last ten days from early sunrise until noon. I knew all the principal figures personally. I had sketched them and talked to them, and as they passed many of them smiled in recognition.

Perhaps the most imposing spectacle of all as it swept past was Rewa. This was quite a gorgeous clump. First came a banner of vivid emerald-green, followed by a warrior on an elephant smothered with huge metal spikes. There were spikes on his breastplate, spikes on his back, spikes on his head, spikes everywhere—a most ferocious-looking creature! Fancy butting into him unawares on a dark night! He seemed every now and then to suffer from a spasm, and the metal spikes rattled almost like kitchen utensils. His was the only figure that might have verged

BOMBAY RETAINERS

on the ridiculous—this spiky warrior's. He shook himself violently as he passed us and blew out his moustache. He knew us, for I had had a long sitting from him only the day before. Close behind him followed a line of elephants—a jumble of jewel-studded howdahs, cloth of gold sweeping the ground, and mahuts in red with pink turbans. One had barely time to take this in before a silver palanquin in the shape of a lion, carried by men in dust-coloured clothes, passed, quickly followed by Rewa irregular troops in green and yellow uniforms and a vivid blue which, amid other conditions, you would have condemned as mercantile.

The next group to attract attention was Orcha. This State was represented by a group of mounted bards playing on the quaintest instruments I have ever seen—most of them two-stringed, others three-stringed. The salmon-coloured gentleman, as they passed, interpreted some of the marvellous things they were chanting. It was all one long poetical rhapsody, he said, on the beauties of their country. One of the bards carried a horn of enormous dimensions. How he ever held it was a marvel to me. It gurgled out the weirdest sounds you could imagine. The only noise that at all resembles it is that which a turkey makes when it has been hurt—badly hurt. It had very much of the turkey character about it. This bard seemed to be playing away on his horn quite independently of his companions; but the salmon-robed gentleman told us that it had been carefully rehearsed and very accurately placed in the orchestra—this gurgle. How brilliant were the horses, and how proudly they marched past, tossing their gorgeous plumes, jingling their silver bells, and walking with a skittish movement, almost a skip! You saw the cobalt-blue shadows dance and tremble on the golden gravel path. These were not trained as ordinary horses are: they were of a special breed, and had been taught to walk with dignity: magnificent creatures, exquisite in form: and as to colour, their owners had simply "let themselves go" and hung them over with every tassel and square inch of cloth of gold they possessed. The trappings were one blaze of colour. Clumps of gold and silver succeeded old-rose and salmon tassels; green-and-gold and vermilion-and-gold saddle-cloths; massive silver anklets; plumes of every colour—the sight was dazzling! Their bodies had been treated as an excuse for decoration, just as a wall would be, or a woman's face. Their tails had been stained, and harmonies had been created on

A FAMOUS DANCING HORSE--BOMBAY CHIEFS' CAMP

THIS horse waltzed round on its hind-legs with quaint dancing steps before the Viceroy on the day of the Retainers' procession.

their bodies. For example, a white horse would have yellow legs and a yellow tail. Many of these "creations" circled round the arena on their hind legs; others literally danced, springing forward in leaps and bounds with their legs gathered under them, and executing curious dancing steps in a way that could never be equalled by any circus horse. Nevertheless, these dancing and prancing horses did not appear ridiculous: there was a certain fitness about them. They are of a special breed that has been trained for generations—not to go through amusing circus acts, but for a very grim and serious purpose, as we have discovered to our own cost. In warfare they were no target: they sprang on one side, or ducked, just like a professional boxer or wrestler. Their riders were able to swing about their great swords, mowing men down by the score. Perhaps they are not the sort of horses that would do for modern warfare; but, nevertheless, they are superb creatures, and as they passed our salmon friend waxed indignant. "You Westerners are spoiling the indigenous stock," he said: "you are destroying the native horse." The man was furious; and, seeing these magnificent fiery creatures, uninitiated person as I am, I could not help feeling that it was a terrible thing to let the breed die out. My neighbour talked in such a depressing way about the influence of the West in this direction that I began to picture the native horse of India extinct and placed as a specimen in the British Museum. Horrible! Fancy seeing this noble arab side by side with the elephant in the hall, and being brushed up day by day by the Museum attendant until there was not a hair left on him; simply living there as a specimen!

In Rajputana we saw real workmen. How devoted the old Raj is to arms! Here were horsemen in chain armour, stern and forbidding of demeanour, clothed in metal from head to foot. The only frivolous touches about them were the golden plumes on their casques and the red-and-white pennons that fluttered on their lances. They took one back to the olden days of battle and bloodshed: they reminded one of boyhood's heroes. How much more awe-inspiring are these mail-clad warriors than our khaki-clad brave soldiers of to-day! One man, the most grim and impressive of the whole warlike contingent, wore a silk sock with a large hole in the heel. Such incongruities are quite usual in India. Rajputana was a warlike group: almost every man carried a weapon of some description. There were squadrons of

QUILTED SOLDIERS OF KISHENGARH

THESE are not dressing-gowns, but padded garments, which form an excellent means of defence against sword-cuts, and are less expensive than armour.

irregular cavalry, and one caught a glimpse of dark fierce eyes through face-guards of polished steel as the famous Jodhpur horsemen passed by. A group of warriors from Kishengarh wore long slate-gray quilted coats, and quilted head-dresses bound with green as a protection from sword-cuts. Rather like dressing-gowns they seemed; but very formidable and inaccessible were these quilted people, with their shields of brass and spears of steel. Bikanir brought quite a new departure in the shape of fifty camel-riders in chain armour, with lemon-yellow saddle-cloths trimmed with apple-green. Both Jodhpur and Bikanir were more or less sad in tone, save for a few touches of colour; and the two groups seemed curiously suggestive of the reddish sandstone of their native country. My salmon neighbour informed me that this reddish sandstone or old Pagwa colour is the colour of the Fakirs, and was matched from the tone of the earth for military reasons, much as we use khaki now. These sad-toned groups were rather a relief: they gave one a rest, and formed the necessary blank spaces after so much brilliant colour. More warriors followed from Rajputana—horsemen with bows and arrows; camel-riders with burnished swivel-guns that shone in the sun like great mirrors; spearmen and matchlock-men on foot; rough-riders and men carrying hand-grenades or rockets; and a crow-catcher in red and silver with green petticoats. Then, there were the Nagas or military ascetics, grotesque figures covered with ochre, performing wild dances. There seemed to be a free fight going on between two of them with spears and shields all the way round the arena.

Palches and all sorts of quaint native vehicles formed an important part of the procession. There were brilliant carts of golden plush hung with violet tassels, the bullocks covered by jewels and silver scales, the drivers dressed in blue, silver, and gold; palanquins of gold and silver embroidery lined with green and old-gold, carried on carmine poles by attendants in red and yellow. Round each carriage and each elephant walked attendants. Men in red and gold carried blazing orange-and-gold fans with gold fringes; others, in purple dresses with orange sashes, carried cloth-of-gold and pink banners; men in yellow and green carried daggers heavily inlaid with gold and jewels, gold and silver clubs, peacocks' feathers, black and gold hung with precious stones, umbrellas of gold, pink, orange, and green, punkhas spotted with gold;

SOME NATIVE VEHICLES

These are marriage-carts, drawn by bullocks.

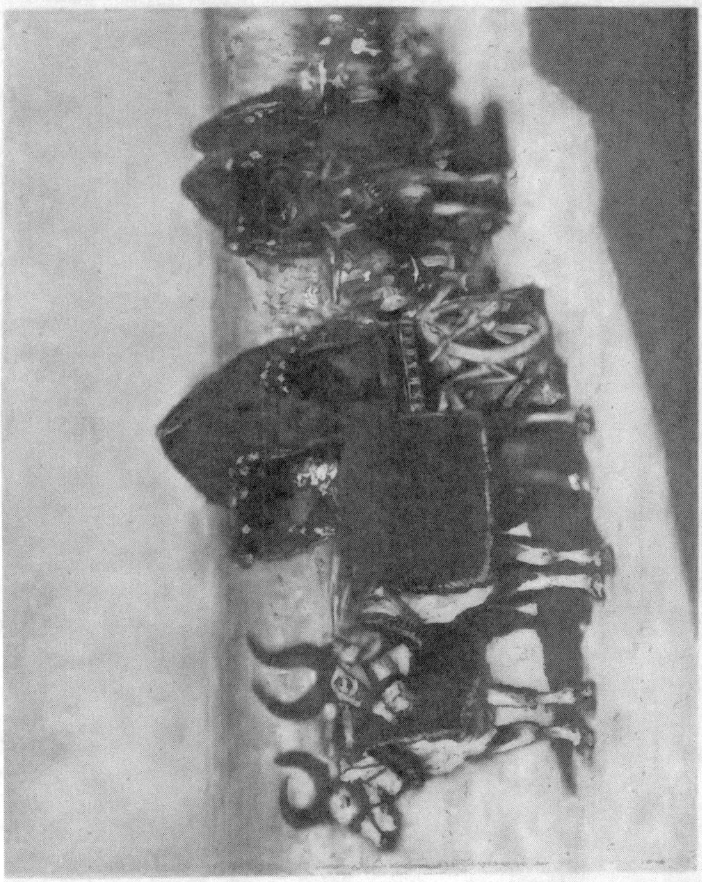

and so they went on in an endless stream too complex to be described.

A huge elephant had a blazing crown of gold upon his head. "That," said the salmon-coloured man, in hushed and reverent accents, "is the *Granth Sahib,* the sacred book of the Sikh brotherhood." "And what is this other book?" I asked, as a gorgeously-dressed horseman appeared, carrying on his arm what seemed to be a large golden book. "I suppose that contains the State secrets?" "Oh dear no," my informant answered, somewhat shocked. "Inside that case is a mirror." Then he explained to me that whenever the Maharaja of Bundi goes visiting, his servant follows behind with his mirror, his comb, his carpet, and his drinking-jar. Whenever the Raja is athirst, he can drink from the jar of the sacred Ganges water. Whenever he meets a chance acquaintance the carpet is spread on the ground, the glass is placed in position, and in the most dignified manner he descends and combs his hair. It is a far cry from Delhi to Burma; but there were the Shans from the farthest corner of their country, dressed in orange-red plush skirts, carmine jackets, and great waving straw hats bent about in fantastic shapes. They walked with great dignity.

Some carried banners, others golden umbrellas; and two stately people held between them a huge gong, hung on a vermilion carved pole, which every now and then gave out a deep mellow booming sound in accord with the stateliness of the procession. I caught a glimpse of them just as they were entering the arena, and I saw the ever-present, active Dunlop Smith dash up on his white arab and say a few words to them. In an instant a blaze of gold shone over their heads: the umbrellas were opened, and looked like a cluster of golden toadstools. I saw the Major afterwards. "I thought they made a better picture so," he said; and there was no doubt about it.

The Punjaub group was perhaps the most uninteresting in the whole review. This was quite a new world altogether—no coats of mail, no prancing horses and crazy bullock-carts, no old emblems illustrating quaint traditions; but lines of soldiers correct and orderly. Western influence showed itself in every detail, from the uniform of the mace-bearers to the shape of their weapons.

"Here come the Sikhs!" cried my salmon-robed neighbour enthusiastically. I turned to see an army of fierce fighting men dressed in dark blue, wearing huge conical turbans decorated with steel

A RETAINER OF THE SHAN CHIEFS

WEARING the Leghorn hat and quaint costume which made the Shan chiefs so different from the Indian retinues, he is a pleasanter, milder, more talkative sort of person.

circlets, and bearing several weapons. These were military devotees. One splendid old fellow, with long white hair and gleaming eyes, rode into the arena on a pony, his feet nearly touching the ground. He was a fanatic. He was clad in a coat of mail, with heavy breastplates back and front; in his hand he held a spear; and as he neared the Viceregal daïs he checked his pony, and, waving his spear on high, in a queer falsetto voice, chanted with great impressiveness the names of the ten Gurus. "Sat Sri Akal!" he shouted. "Only the Nameless One is real." On the anniversary of Govind Sinh all the Sikhs went in a solemn procession to his tomb to do homage to his name.

The day before the ceremony this old fanatic came to Dunlop Smith, and said, "Sahib, I have got a great idea." The Major, who is always prepared to feel with his people in any of their little eccentricities, smiled, and expressed himself as anxiously waiting to hear. "To-morrow is to be the great ceremony," said the old fellow very earnestly, "and I, a devotee, a Sikh, am going to attend with my pony. Now, Sahib, I have decided to make a Sikh of my pony. I have made a pair of drawers for him, and he is to wear them on the great day." The explanation is that every Sikh is compelled to carry five things on his person, and one of them is a pair of drawers. Thus, in order to become a member of the sacred brotherhood, that wretched pony was to career off to the Retainers' ceremony in a white cotton leg-gear! Of course, Major Dunlop Smith was ready-witted. "What a splendid idea!" he said. "I am so glad you thought of it." When the poor old man appeared, and we saw the back view of the pony in his white drawers going out of the gate, the whole camp was convulsed, and we had to rush indoors lest he should hear.

The retainers of the young Maharaja of Patiala were very gorgeous. There were stately elephants richly caparisoned and remarkable for the beauty of their howdahs, an enormous silver sedan chair, and Patiala's own marvellous gold-and-silver state carriage drawn by four white horses and upholstered in pale pink. It was one of the most splendid items in the procession, and the crowd cheered. The young ruler looked excited and pleased; but, as fate would have it, just as the carriage passed the Viceregal daïs one of the horses jibbed, and, despite all the pushings, whippings, and persuasions, refused to move. Patiala, a handsome boy dressed

IN THE RETAINERS' PROCESSION

in brilliant blue and hung about with pearls and jewels worth a fabulous sum, was sitting directly in front of us. Another young ruler sat next him. Patiala's arm was thrown round his companion's shoulder, and as the carriage broke down I noticed his effort not to show emotion. He was so young that he could not entirely control his feelings: there was a nervous twitch in his face, and he kept looking towards his carriage. At last, after five minutes or so of vain exertions to make the horses move, they were taken out from their traces and led round the arena. It was marvellous to watch the indifferent manner in which young Patiala laughed and chatted with his friend, who was fighting his disappointment bravely.

As the procession passed, my friend in the salmon dress began to point out various interesting and celebrated people sitting in the arena of the crowded amphitheatre. There were the picturesque figures of the Chiefs from the Shan States in the old court dress of the Kings of Burma. With their high conical headgear of pure gold blazing with emeralds and diamonds, and their gold-winged robes, they looked like walking pagodas. Stolidly and impassively they watched the gorgeous retinues of the Chiefs of India pass by. Many of them had never been to India before; yet they sat there quite unmoved, as though it were the most natural and everyday occurrence. The Maharaja of Cooch Behar was dressed in a magnificent costume with jewels — a striking contrast to Maharao Bundhi in his workmanlike dress. Sir Pratap Singh, honorary Colonel of the Imperial Cadet Corps, was a gallant figure. My salmon friend waxed eloquent on the subject of his virtues. "Ah," he said, "but he is a great soldier! He is proud of his C.B. for Tirah — prouder of that order than of all his other decorations. All the rest were given him because he was a Maharaja; but his C.B. was given him because he was a soldier."

Maharaja Nhama was there, that splendid, soldierly old Sikh, with his clear-cut features and long white beard: an ascetic-looking man. All seemed to be anxious to impress him with the Retainers' show: they did not want him to think that it suggested a circus or in any way lacked dignity. He was dying, and he knew it. This was the last procession he would see, and it was only by stupendous will-power that he was able to join in the Durbar celebrations. Even now Maharaja Nhama goes out hawking on his favourite horse, which is full of fire.

THE STATE ENTRY: A DISTINGUISHED MAHARAJA

One of the elephants who, by its amazing revelation of splendour, struck all Delhi dumb with wonder.

British officials have often tried to persuade him to ride a tamer beast; but Maharaja Nhama is such a stickler for etiquette and dignity that, so long as he has an ounce of energy left, he will appear as a king should appear. Indeed, one could not picture this splendid old man riding anything but this especial kingly steed.

ON THE ALIPUR ROAD

The natives during the Durbar were so overcome with the magnificence and splendour of the proceedings that they could do nothing but stand by the roadside all day long in wide-eyed, wide-mouthed wonder.

VI

THE REVIEW OF THE TROOPS

VICEROY REVIEWING THE TROOPS

VI

THE REVIEW OF THE TROOPS

THIS was Lord Kitchener's day, the day for the military. The troops had played a prominent part in all the great ceremonies; but this was a day set apart for them alone, when they had an opportunity of showing themselves in all their splendid strength. Thirty thousand British troops were gathered together in Imperial Delhi—a glorious sight, a sight to make our rivals tremble. The natives themselves were never more impressed than at this Military Review. Weapons and fighting men invariably appeal to the native mind, and this tremendous display gave them an idea of the power of the British Raj.

Not only did the Review impress the natives: also it impressed the whole world, or, rather, the representatives from almost all over the world who were gathered together on the grand stands to witness the display. To see native troops parading shoulder to shoulder with the British, wearing the same uniforms, marching under the same colours, each and all filled with the same fealty to the King Emperor, could not but impress the world with the strength of our hold on India.

It was a blazing day. The sun flashed on the bayonets and accoutrements of the apparently unending line of troops drawn up about a quarter of a mile from the flagstaff and waiting for the arrival of the Viceroy. There were two enormous stands —one for the Viceroy's guests and high officials, and the other for the general public. Almost every man was in uniform; the stands formed a blaze of scarlet and gold; while all round the Review ground natives thronged in their multi-coloured clothes. Surrounded by an exceptionally brilliant staff, Lord Kitchener was stationed facing the flagstaff on a magnificent charger. At half-past ten precisely thirty-one guns were fired. It was the Royal Salute; and Lord Curzon, wearing morning dress, was seen approaching on horseback. He was accompanied by the Duke of Connaught, a soldierly figure in Field-Marshal's uniform, and the Duke of Hesse in dark blue. Preceding the procession was a small detachment of the Viceregal

NATIVE HORSEMEN IN THE REVIEW OF NATIVE RETAINERS

bodyguard in their scarlet-and-gold; following them were the Imperial Cadets, magnificent as usual. The troops fired a Royal Salute as His Excellency reached the saluting point; the National Anthem was played; the Royal Standard was unfurled. Lady Curzon and the Duke of Connaught were driven in their carriage to the enclosure.

The march-past was headed by Lord Kitchener's staff, Sir George Wolseley, Sir Bindon Blood, Sir Robert Low, and the Commander-in-Chief riding apart, accompanied by a single orderly. As he passed the Viceroy, the Commander-in-Chief saluted slowly and ceremoniously, and handed him the parade state of the forces. It was an imposing spectacle—the Viceroy, the Duke of Connaught, Lord Kitchener, the heads of the Staff, and the native Rulers, who one by one, as they led on their troops, circled round and took up their positions by the Viceroy. It was one of the most picturesque groups of soldiers you could possibly imagine—one of the most mixed and varied. There was the workmanlike figure of Lord Kitchener, keen and absorbed; a native servant continually carrying messages backwards and forwards; the Duke of Connaught in scarlet; the Grand Duke of Hesse in dark blue; the soldierly young Maharaja of Idar;

young Patiala, a gallant little figure in salmon-and-gold; the ancient Maharaja of Nabha on his fiery arab, bent and old, yet soldierly and dignified still; and countless others. The Viceroy, in dull-coloured frock-coat and gray helmet, was the only neutral figure in the brilliant group.

The march-past was wonderful. The men moved like some magnificent machine. Nearly every troop of cavalry was perfect, never deviating a hair's-breadth from the straight line. Some regiments were more or less coldly received; others were cheered loudly and wildly from the moment the first pennon fluttered in the distance until the last horse disappeared from view. The Anglo-Indians among the audience were deeply interested. They knew every regiment and every commander. Slighting or enthusiastic remarks were heard constantly as to the horses, the men, their manner of riding, and other matters interesting to a soldier, but unintelligible to a civilian. The patriotic excitement was tremendous. Men forgot themselves, and spoke or shouted out their thoughts on the impulse of the moment. Just before the Ninth Lancers passed the atmosphere was electric. The people were quiet—quite quiet—expectant. As the regiment came into view the whole stand rose and

ARMED CAMEL RIDERS FROM BIKANIR

THEY remind one of a page from Scott—the friends and foes of one's boyhood.

cheered itself hoarse; women waved their handkerchiefs, many of them not knowing why they did it; men flourished their sticks and shouted bravos. That mighty cheer must have been heard for miles around.

I was down close by the saluting point, and could study the Viceroy. His face was set and immobile as a flint; but just as the Ninth Lancers advanced to within thirty or forty yards of the flagstaff his horse began to be restive, to fidget and circle round, showing that, though the man's exterior was calm and unruffled, he was inwardly anxious and nervous. Lord Curzon must have made some slight nervous movement, and the horse felt it, as well-bred horses do. It seems a little thing, this; but to us who were watching the tension was so great that it appeared important at the moment. There is no doubt about it: the fact of the Viceroy's own guests standing up and cheering showed exceedingly little tact. Even though they may have questioned his treatment of the Ninth Lancers, this was hardly a fitting moment to give way to their feelings. It was a distinct stab at the Viceroy. Here was Lord Curzon, who had taken a certain measure from conviction. He would have equal justice between native and British; these murders had been increasing; and there came a moment when he must put his foot down firmly. He did what from his standpoint he knew to be absolutely right. For his own guests to choose that moment to insult him did seem hard and ungenerous.

The regiments passed by in alphabetical order—an unending stream of perfectly equipped, faultless lines. To mention all would be impossible. Those who attracted most attention were the Hyderabad Lancers, magnificent riders; the Royal Field Artillery, marching past in perfect order, distinguished batteries having fought through the South African campaign; the Royal Irish Rifles, whose popularity was quite extraordinary; the Dragoon Guards; the Hussars; the Imperial Service Cavalry; the Alwar Lancers, led by their young chief, a splendid horseman; the Gurkha regiments; the King's Royal Rifles; the Sappers and Miners, with pontoons and balloons; the Bikanir Camel Corps, led by the young Maharaja of Bikanir; the Gordon Highlanders; the Argyll and Sutherlands. These last were perhaps most popular of all. "Don't they look sweet?" the ladies cried. "How prettily their kilts swing as they march along." "It is curious how popular

HIS HIGHNESS THE MAHARAJA OF PATIALA

The little eleven-year-old Maharaja bore himself with great dignity and gravity and saluted the Viceroy with his little sword with all the composure of the oldest of his warriors.

the Highland regiments are with the ladies," I heard one man remark; "but I must say they are splendid fellows," he added grudgingly. The Sikhs made a gallant show. So did the Madras Infantry, the Welsh regiments, the Bombay Light Horse, and the Jats. Perhaps the greatest applause of all was accorded to Patiala, a soldierly little figure bearing himself magnificently at the head of his Lancers and riding on a white pony. He was in a salmon-and-gold dress and wore a pale green turban. The young Maharaja rode with surprising dignity, head erect and his little sword proudly drawn,—a slight figure among so many grown and bearded men. As he passed the Viceroy he saluted as well and as easily as any veteran there, and the people on the grand stands clapped and shouted until they could shout no more. The ladies' hearts with one accord went out to him. "Isn't he a dear?" "Isn't he a darling?" they cried. He was a mere child, only eleven years old. The Maharaja of Nabha, an elderly gentleman,—but, oh, how proud and dignified as he marched by to-day on his fiery horse at the head of his Infantry—followed young Patiala. The contrast as they circled round and took their respective places among the groups of officers was extraordinary—

the little boy and the old chief Nabha: the one whose life was only just beginning, and the other whose life was so nearly completed.

One could not see the troops in the distance. They were covered with clouds of dust as though with a gauzy veil. Now and then a horseman would flash out of the haze; but just as suddenly thousands would disappear. As they drew near it was extraordinary how little dust they created, and as they passed the Viceroy there was practically none. Heavy mountain batteries passed; yet there was hardly any dust. The people on the stands wondered how the miracle had been achieved. We by the flagstaff knew. All along the line for almost a mile running parallel with the troops, a trench had been dug and filled with water. All along the trench were stationed bheesties (water-carriers) with brown skin bags filled with water. There were hundreds of them. You couldn't see them from the stands; but directly a regiment passed which created any dust, swarms of these coolies ran out and in an instant spread themselves all over the ground, sprinkling as they went. They looked like part of the earth themselves: their bodies were brown, their faces were brown, and their skins were brown. They did

ARMOURED HORSES

their work with rapidity and dexterity. I thought them extremely picturesque.

We did not stay long on the stand, but wandered about on the Review ground watching these coolies. I found Mr. Raven Hill, instead of sketching the Headquarters Staff, hard at work on a group of the bheesties; and I could not help thinking, as I looked, how much more picturesque they were, and how much better they grouped themselves, these sons of the soil, men of no more consequence than the lizards in the sand.

It was interesting to watch the ladies with their cameras. How keen they were! Many of them employed staff officers to carry their kodaks, and came right out in the broiling sun down by the trench in order to take snapshots of the soldiers as they passed. It was amusing to see well-known London Society women completely forgetting themselves in the anxiety of the moment, and running full-tilt down the slope to get a snapshot of a native ruler or a native horseman. The kodak fiend seemed to have settled on all the visitors at Delhi and made them its own. There was nothing that quiet, dignified people would not do for the sake of getting a good snapshot. You would see a clergyman creeping stealthily under the cordon, and across the space of ground set apart for the Viceroy and officials, until he came within six yards of them, and then snap his kodak in their faces. He only wanted a pair of list slippers and a dark lantern to complete his burglarious appearance. Many people from the stands shouted out that the clergyman blocked their line of vision, and that he was to be taken away; but he was not hindered.

The last event of the day was almost the best of all. When the Infantry had withdrawn, the Cavalry and Artillery formed up a quarter of a mile away in three separate divisions—three great masses of men parallel with the stands. It was a splendid force, one that would sweep all before it and could not be checked. At a given signal the whole mass advanced towards us at full gallop, one plunging wall of horses and metal and wheels. There was a great rumble and the cracking of many whips. For a moment we held our breath: it seemed as though that tearing mass could never stop: it must sweep us away, stands and all. In an instant, however, and with a precision beautiful to see, the troops halted, turned about, and galloped off the plain. It was perhaps one of the most successful manœuvres of the whole successful day.

ONE OF THE MOST PICTURESQUE
GROUPS IN THE RETAINERS' PROCESSION

Getting home was a difficulty. The crush was tremendous. It took us a good three hours to get back. The police wrung their hands, and in despair gave up organising the traffic. Three-quarters of the time we were standing still; every carriage had the horse's head of the following carriage thrust in at the back. We fed the same horse with biscuits all the way back. It got to know us, and we were there long enough for the creature to become quite fond of us. You can get an idea by this of the compactness of the mass. You would see a distinguished English officer trying to use his authority to cause a move-on; but it was absolutely useless. Peppery Anglo-Indian officials grew purple in the face and swore at their drivers; the best-tempered people became irritable; the dust seemed to enter every pore of one's skin; it spoilt the ladies' dresses, filled their hair and eyes and mouth; nearly every face was covered with a pocket-handkerchief.

VII

THE PRESS CAMP

AN ELEPHANT AND RETAINERS FROM BIKANIR

The jhool upon this elephant and the embroidery on the velvet is worth a king's ransom.

VII

THE PRESS CAMP

THE Press Camp was far away the most brilliant at the Durbar. It was universally acknowledged that the food was better, the wine better, everything better — most notably the conversation and the table-talk. From the moment I moved with my kit from Number One Camp to the Press Camp I was in a changed atmosphere. I found myself among workers, real workers — not people who worked occasionally and tried to combine work with gaiety, but really hard workers. You might come in at night at any hour, sometimes daybreak, and still you would see almost every tent illuminated, and catch a glimpse through every doorway of a bent figure in shirt-sleeves in the midst of a pile of papers, with a green-shaded electric light pouring down upon the bowed head and swiftly-flying pen. Mind you, these men would be up again at five or six o'clock in the morning, with very little rest in between. They would have breakfasted and be on the scene of action before the more luxurious Durbarites had thought of taking their *chota hasri.*

Hard work they had, too, to recall their impressions of that marvellous Durbar. It is not that the impressions were lacking; but how is a man to succeed when the printers in London are waiting and he has only a few hours to convey any idea to the British public of, say, the Chandni Chauk on a particularly bright day, when not only would the crowds be clothed in gorgeous turbans and rich attire, but also the colours would change like the moving glasses of a kaleidoscope—where you would see figures unwinding themselves, unwrapping portions of their garments —perhaps a violet cloak thrown off revealing citron-yellow underneath, and so on, and so on, continually throwing off colours and revealing others? And these colours seemed to reflect colours into other colours. This will sound strange to any one who has never seen it; but I state a fact. For example, you would see a gentleman floating down the street in a yellow turban and dress so brilliant that all the blues

A RETAINER FROM CENTRAL INDIA

became greens at his approach. What resource has painter or writer to compete with things like these? Merely a palette in one hand; pen and ink in the other! Small wonder that they become dazed, colour-blind, exhausted. There are occasions when words are useless and pigment is but mud.

The correspondents and artists were all very charming people. There was a cameraderie among them, and a sympathy one with another through failures and successes, that was truly delightful. With all their hard work, they never seemed to lose their appetite for social gatherings. They loved these little gaieties, and enjoyed themselves during their leisure hours like a troop of light-hearted schoolboys. Always asking one another to dinner, and forming small parties at the separate tables, every one knew everybody else; and they seemed as though they had been there for years. It was like one big family.

One always got the latest information at the Press Camp. Nothing occurred but that these astute people were well posted as to its every detail. From the moment one entered the Press Camp one seemed to be in the centre of everything.

Our first meal at the Camp was luncheon; and at least a dozen different correspondents came up and offered suggestions, and showed a keen and kindly interest in us. Among the most helpful was Mr. Chirrol of *The Times.* There was no jealousy in the Press Camp, no anxiety to outdo one another: everything was talked out, and every one was ready to help. You would often see two or three artists dash out of their tents and fly across to the tent of a journalist opposite with pictures they had just painted: the journalist was to give them titles, so as to help the pictures from the literary standpoint. Then, again, it was not unusual to see three or four journalists circled round Mr. Melton Prior or Mr. Jacomb Hood, getting them to describe details of dress and the colouring of different scenes.

Everything of interest that had occurred during the day was discussed during dinner. Journalists and draughtsmen moved round the fire in the luxurious drawing-room and chatted until all hours of the night. The correspondent of *The Daily Telegraph* was specially brilliant as a conversationalist. He and Mr. Chirrol and Mr. Sheldon were clever talkers. Then, there would be the interesting and quaint asides of Mr. Melton Prior,

A RETAINER FROM ALWAR

ONE of the horses for which the State is famous.

remarks which had never anything to do with the subject in question but were always very amusing. He spent nearly all his spare time getting his hair cut.

There was a great excitement in the Camp after the Military Review, the last event of the Durbar; and one and all were furious with the behaviour of some of the Viceroy's guests, who had the exceedingly bad taste to cheer the Ninth Lancers. They talked it over until two or three o'clock in the morning. One and all agreed that it was a cruel stab at Lord Curzon, and that, no matter how strong their sympathies might have been with the Ninth, to cheer in the presence of their host was inexcusable.

The Viceroy quite won the hearts of the journalists the day that he visited their Camp. He spoke a few pleasant words to each of them. They all came away pleased; although each man felt that he might have said something a little different, having just missed saying the right thing —while some had said nothing at all.

At our first dinner in the Press Camp we were surrounded by journalists and literally pounced upon for new words with which to express colour. There were two or three artists there; but they had seen so much that they were colour-blind. Even although the Durbar ceremonies had only been going on for two or three days when we arrived, the painters had painted and the journalists had written themselves out. It was always the same thing. You would see a man rushing off to the telegraph station with a cable that he was sending to his paper. "Look here," he would say: "just look at it! Isn't it dry stuff! And I have got to send that off! It is nothing at all—nothing at all! I say that things are 'glorious' and 'gorgeous' and 'wonderful'; but it doesn't convey any impression of the real thing to those at home." All were depressed more or less by the futility of their work. The black-and-white artists showed their distress in the same way. They were limp, unable to give any impression at all. They felt as I did, and as we all did, that it was impossible. During my first few days at the Camp, in the course of conversation I happened suddenly to say two words that expressed the gorgeous colouring of the Durbar, "clean-cut and gem-like." These apparently innocent words of mine had the effect of a human body thrown to the lions. They were pounced upon instantly and devoured! It was only for the first day or

SHAN RETAINERS CARRYING A BRASS GONG

A Burmese gong which was sounded during the procession, and which gave out a peculiarly rich and resonant note.

two that I was able to think of new adjectives. After that I was as completely played out as themselves.

There is no doubt about it: the journalists were well cared for in Delhi. In fact, they were in clover, and had everything they wanted. They had bicycles, horses, and carriages, and the best seats for every ceremony. It was really a marvellously good time for them—almost like a picnic on a large scale, except for the excessively hard work.

SHAN CHIEFS WATCHING THE DURBAR

One of these chiefs has fifty wives, and is known as "The Flower round whom the Butterflies flutter."

VIII

THE RAJPUTANA CAMP

A RETAINER OF RAJGARH

VIII

THE RAJPUTANA CAMP

ONE of the first things we determined to do on arriving at Delhi was to occupy ourselves with the Native Chiefs' Camps, and devote every morning to them. I was lucky enough to come in touch with the very man who could help me more than any one in Delhi, Major Dunlop Smith. He entered into the spirit of my work, and immediately wrote letters to the officers in charge of the different camps telling them to be prepared on certain stated mornings to parade all their chiefs' retinues. This meant a great economy of time. Each day when I arrived at the different camps I found them in a whirl of excitement, and each day I had a magnificent rehearsal of the great Retainers' show that was to follow. One of the first camps visited was the Rajputana Camp. We spent a whole day there. In a way it was perhaps one of the most interesting of all: because of the infinite variety of the costume and the great kindness of the officer in charge, Major Minchin.

At daybreak we had started out in our yellow tonga, taking with us the map we always carried and which never seemed to be of any use. It had taken us about three hours to find the Camp, which was only half an hour's distance off. The route had been elaborately explained to the driver and to me, and I checked him throughout the whole journey by my map. We had constantly stopped at cross roads to examine the sign-posts, and questioned the passers-by; and in the end, after two long hours, we had managed so successfully that we did not know where we were.

It was then that Major Dunlop Smith appeared on the scene. He certainly was our good angel at all times, and we hailed him with joy. We told him that we had lost our way, and were looking for the Rajputana Camp. He smiled. "Do you know," he said, "you are coming in exactly the opposite direction?" "To ensure your safety I will lend you two of my Sikhs to act as guides." Instantly two magnificent persons in blue and steel left his side and galloped in front of our little tonga. Our carroty-haired driver was on the

A CAMEL RIDER FROM KOTA

THESE huge animals passed by quite noiselessly except for the jingling of their trappings.

point of bursting with pride. He was always a proud man, and in the habit of carelessly slashing the natives about him with his whip. With these two mounted soldiers riding in front of us, their pennons fluttering and their armour glistening in the morning sun, this half-nude carroty-bearded person was as proud as a peacock. We were safely escorted to the Rajputana Camp, and Major Minchin took us in hand.

There was a tremendous bustle and preparation going on—lines of elephants in gorgeous trappings, camels, horses, and hundreds of retainers—and we felt a little embarrassed as we realised that this tremendous show, which must have taken hours to prepare, had been arranged entirely for our benefit. The great array of retainers was grouped on a vast plain some minutes distant, and I shall never forget the sight they presented as we rode up. There was the great wide-spreading plain, stretching as far as we could see, and in the middle all these hundreds of jewel-bedecked men and animals. It was like a handful of jewels sprinkled on silver sand—a veritable treasure island in a silver sea. We studied the different States one by one. It was marvellous to watch them as they marched past—some galloping, others flouncing by on horses that walked on their hind legs, and all sorts of curious things happening constantly. One thing that appealed to us as being rather extraordinary was that nearly every one of these men seemed to occupy an important position in his particular State. Sometimes, when I wanted one of them to move, I would catch him by the arm and lead him away. Afterwards, to my consternation, I discovered that he was Commander-in-Chief of the Forces! There was no difficulty in getting these people to sit: they were all only too anxious.

A most interesting group was Jaipur. There was one magnificent figure, a man, on an elephant covered with gorgeous trappings, carrying the State standard, along with two more on horseback, one carrying a silver trident and the other kettledrums. Then, in the same State there was a group of elephants carrying the insignia conferred by the Mogul Emperors, together with ten horsemen in chain armour. These chain-armoured people, very grim and warlike, looked as though they had stepped from out of the Middle Ages. Their head-dress was of brass, with a nodding golden plume; their armour was of shining steel; and in their hands they carried lances with red-and-white pennons. There were all kinds of

JAIPUR ELEPHANTS

RETURNING home tired after the day's work, and longing no doubt to be rid of their burdensome finery.

warriors in Rajputana, each group more gorgeous and extraordinary than the last. Some of the irregular cavalry of Kota were very rich in colouring. Each man seemed to have been allowed to follow his own feelings with regard to the colour of his dress. Many of them were armed with swords and old shields. Kota, perfect jumble of colour, was interesting material for the artist. There were rough-riders, mace-bearers, umbrella-bearers, with banners of all shapes and colours. In Kishengarh there was a whole regiment of horsemen in chain armour. They carried an old-world atmosphere. In this same State quilt-coated warriors had been prepared for us. These were men with slate-gray quilted dressing-gowns and quilted head-dresses, with protectors for their ears. This curious feather-bed armour was supposed to protect them from sword-cuts. Strangely enough, these men did not look ridiculous. There was a certain fitness about them.

In the Rajputana groups the colouring was gorgeous; but at the same time the costumes were eminently practical. These people were all warriors. One could see that at a glance. There was no suggestion of the circus about them. Everything they wore was designed for work.

Even the performing horses from Alwar, which passed before us on their hind legs, almost waltzing as they walked, did not look at all out of place. They had been trained for a very practical purpose. In the Alwar group there were men on elephants, with old matchlock guns, and fourteen men on foot, some with silver spears and some with maces. The Alwar group was particularly interesting from the artistic standpoint—warriors on elephants in old costumes, and everything out of date. They had worn these dresses all their lives, and one felt more in the Alwar State than in any other that this was the last time the men of the Orient would be seen by Westerners in these ancient garbs. Soon the old order would give place to new.

The painting of the horses was very quaint. They were nearly all adorned just as the elephants were. For example, there would be a white horse with his legs and half his tail stained a brilliant yellow. There was only one animal that looked ridiculous in the Alwar group: that was an elephant carrying a pair of chandeliers with candles attached to his tusks.

There was one group where some very clever trick-riding was done. One man rode on his horse at all angles. Sometimes he rode suspended from

A PERFORMING HORSE FROM THE ALWAR STATE

To help the colour scheme, the legs and tail of this horse have been stained.

its tail, sometimes underneath it; and all the time the horse was galloping at full tilt, while we held our breath in fear. I have never seen such marvellous trick-riding in any circus in Europe. While this performance was going on my attention was distracted by the sight of a man carrying a long stick with, on the end of it, something curious which he handled carefully. I inquired what this was, and discovered that it was a rocket. There was an entire regiment of people with rockets. They were very formidable people, who held an important position in battle. They fired the rockets off during a skirmish. No one seemed to know exactly what they did now, or why they were there; but these old gentlemen with the rockets were ready on an emergency to scare the enemy and put them off the scent.

One of the most beautiful elephants in Rajputana was in Bikanir. This animal bore shining silver scales that rattled as he walked. Then, there was that beautiful State chariot which I have talked of before—the State chariot drawn by two bullocks bedecked in silver chain-work, as beautifully finished as a lady's purse, and adorned with innumerable tassels of old-rose and silver.

In the Kotah group there were fifteen religious

military ascetics. Some of them, as they paraded before us, held mock fights. Smeared with brown earth, and painted in stripes of yellow ochre, they were scarcely dressed at all: in fact, the costume of these gentlemen consisted entirely of stripes. They were extremely comic in their gesture, and we remarked directly we saw them that if they behaved in that way on the great day, they would bring down the house. They reminded me of two fowls when I noted the way they crept up and circled round one another with terrible war-like gestures, raising their arms to strike a terrific blow—a blow which was never struck,—and then the whole pantomime would begin over again.

The handling of the Great Delhi Durbar was a stupendous work. When you think of the number of special trains it must have taken to bring these Chiefs and their retinues to the scene, one wonders how it can ever have been accomplished with so few mistakes. One State alone of the Rajputana group took three special trains to bring them to Delhi—not counting the camels and the mules and the horses, which walked all the way from their native country. Jaipur, Jodhpur, and many others all came down from their magnificent palaces in the hills, palaces

AN ELEPHANT FROM THE SANDY WASTES OF RAJPUTANA

of marble and those grim fastnesses which were stormed so many times by Mogul Emperors, but were never taken—palaces in which the romance of India and Indian life is being played day after day. The Rajputana chiefs have in their veins the proudest and the oldest blood in the world. The Maharana of Udaipur claims a descent of one hundred and forty generations before Agamemnon. The State of Udaipur was held by his ancestors long before any country in Europe had a nationality. Think of that! It almost makes one's brain whirl.

When Rajputana had unravelled all its glories before our eyes, leaving us faint and weary and almost colour-blind, we left that dazzling plain with its thousands of gorgeous retainers, and went to call on one of the residents in the Camp. It was refreshing to sit in Mrs. Stratton's, the drawing-room of the beautiful Mrs. Stratton, who certainly deserves that title, being one of the most beautiful women in India. Her tent was quite the most artistically arranged that I had seen in Delhi. The reason was very obvious. The owner was a painter; he had exhibited pictures in the New Gallery and in many places. They told me that they had been entertaining the Viceroy lately, and Captain Stratton described some of the shooting parties which Lord Curzon attended. One day, he said, the Viceroy, out shooting, found himself, except for a few coolies, alone in a wood, in which Captain Stratton came upon him. His knowledge of the native language was extremely limited, and he was endeavouring to persuade the coolies to move on in a certain direction. He only knew one phrase, which he repeated continually, and that meant that they were not to stir! Captain and Mrs. Stratton spoke of the Viceroy—as indeed every one in India spoke—as being a man of broad sympathies and simple nature, interested in the smallest details of his great office.

On our way home, we passed through the native quarter of old Delhi, where the streets swarm with people. There were no English officers, no tourists, no signs of the Delhi Durbar. The Durbar might have been thousands of miles away for all one saw of it there. The natives moved about sleepily, lazily; half of them were sleeping on the wayside, or sitting and staring at nothing all day long. I doubt if the majority of them knew or cared a fig about the Coronation of His Majesty King Edward. Down the middle of the broad road was an avenue of giant old trees,

A SIKH SPEAR-BEARER

His turban is stuck full of war implements, and he comes from the golden temple of Amritsar.

throwing a flickering pattern, like delicate lace-work, of sun and shadow on the road beneath. On either side of the street were crazy houses, brown-stained, and ramshackle, keeping together as though by a miracle; they were like children's card-houses, all on a slant and "tipsy." The balconies to the windows were of brilliant blues and greens; and there were striped red-and-white awnings, torn and faded, kept up on either side by slender sticks. I saw a child step out on to the balcony with a naked brown baby in her arms, and I trembled for its safety as she trod on the frail old woodwork. Down in the streets the shops were a blaze of colour. Curious shops they were, high up off the ground like berths in a steamer; and strange things were for sale—fritters and blocks of pudding stuff, and sweet-meats, brown, fried cakes, lumps of dried meat hung up in strings, chillies, oranges, and all kinds of delicacies. Some of these shops are eating-houses; men, women, children, and even babies sit outside in the road, munching and tearing at unsavoury food. The street was brown, the houses were brown, and most of the people were brown; for they were nearly all poor, and dressed in a kind of soiled linen. Still, there were the vivid patches of colour, the reds and vermilions and yellows and greens of the more clothed people —which were like a handful of flowers thrown on silver sand. You saw women in blood-red dresses —the regular Indian red of the pictures one has seen of Nautch girls. Here was the Nautch girl to the life, and it was evidently her work-a-day attire. Her accordion-pleated skirt swung to and fro as she walked; her bare arms and feet were decorated with clumpy gold and jewelled bracelets; there were jewels on her clothes, in her ears and nose. She was every bit as beautiful as the Nautch girl of pictorial tradition. Her features were just as aquiline, her big eyes just as flashing; but she was not dancing to the sound of sweet music. On her head she carried a large sort of double-barrelled brass drinking-vase, or else, perhaps, supported on her shoulder, in company with another woman, a long pole, on which was suspended a long kind of palanquin—one did not know what it contained, but it was closely covered. What magnificent types one sees in the streets!—men clothed in a few dirty rags with the features and bearing of Apollo. They might have been young gods instead of penniless peasants, by their column-like necks,

A KASHMIRI SOLDIER

ONE of the peculiarities in the dress of these Kashmiri soldiers is that the inner and outer turban must always harmonise.

their hair growing low on their foreheads, their flashing black eyes, their shapely limbs, and the haughty pose of their heads. They were all more or less handsome; and how lazy! They sat about for hour upon hour, most of them, as though they had nothing in the world to do but simply gaze. Boys were plaguing the drivers of empty carriages as they passed, and inciting them by all the means in their power to get off their perch and use the whip. They often got a smart whack; but the fun of the thing was quite worth it in their opinion. It was extraordinary how they created excitements out of nothing. I saw two small boys evidently planning something wicked. Soon they began to fight and yell and dash one another on the ground, one of them pretending to set his teeth in the other's arm. Every one dropped work and bustled up; and soon a great crowd collected, the traffic was suspended, and some soldiers stopped and tried to separate the brats. Suddenly both the urchins got up, smiled round on the audience they had collected, and made off as fast as they could go.

We drove through the native quarter and back to the Press Camp to prepare for a great function.

A SOLDIER OF HIS HIGHNESS DOGRA SOWAR

IX

THE PUNJAUB CAMP

BODYGUARD OF HIS HIGHNESS. DOGRA SOWAR KASHMIR

THE uniform of these men is much like the ancient French cuirassiers—the man on the left with his sword drawn is an officer.

IX

THE PUNJAUB CAMP

WE spent several days at the Punjaub Camp. The great help given us by Major Dunlop Smith made everything easy. He prepared for us not only the Punjaub groups but also Kashmir and Baluchistan. On the first morning at the Punjaub Camp we found that Mr. Jacomb Hood and Mr. Raven Hill had arrived before us. As we came up they were sketching the two holy men from Amritsar. On that first day we did very little work. Most of our time was spent in being taken round by a native officer to see the treasures of the various States. We saw gold howdahs by the dozen, State tents, solid silver chains, gold-embroidered carpets, and marvellous old pictures, until our brains whirled with the magnificence of it all. Another day Major Dunlop Smith handed us over to an officer in charge of the Kashmir

Camp, a native who spoke English perfectly and acted as umbrella-bearer as well as interpreter.

One by one the different Kashmir types were trotted out before us to be sketched. There were men in armour, looking like old French cuirassiers, with dark blue uniforms, breast-plates, brass helmets, and mailed gloves. It was a splendid opportunity. Strings of these people were brought out to stand in the sun firmly and steadily while I sketched them. They were nearly all types with beautiful features, and they were dressed in the most gorgeous costumes—emerald-green sheathed swords, purple brocade trimmed with gold, and all the richest colours you can imagine. There were no two alike, and each man seemed to have used his own feeling with regard to colour. Many of them were retainers of His Highness Dogra Sowar. One man came before me, a soldier with a heron's plume in his turban; and he was so magnificent that I promptly made a study of him as he stood there. He wore a blood-red turban trimmed with gold, in which the heron's plume waved bravely. Over his cobalt-blue coat was thrown a mantle of purple trimmed with gold; there was a gold belt and pouch of gold;

A KASHMIRI PUNDAT

The splash of orange on the forehead of this high official is a caste mark, which he washes off and repaints every morning.

round his neck hung an orange ribbon decorated with rubies and emeralds, as well as strings of pearls, tightly wound; and two large and perfect pearls adorned his ears. He was a soldier. There were no others exactly like him. Some were equally gorgeous; but they were all different in get-up. A Kashmiri pundat was all white, with silver slippers. The only touch of vivid colour about him was his caste mark; that was of a rich orange, and placed in the middle of his forehead. The umbrella-bearer, the gentleman who was explaining things, informed us in a stage whisper that the pundat washed the orange caste mark off and painted it on again every morning. This Kashmir group was especially interesting because of the extraordinary variety of the types. There were men from the hills—men whose homes were spread over tremendous tracts of country; men who had never seen one another before, now brought into close contact; hill shepherds—curious people, with gentle, sad faces, and sad-coloured dresses of gray wool, with furs, and red untanned leather boots.

After we had exhausted the Kashmiri groups we went back to the Punjaub Camp. We spent many days in this delightful place. There was gaiety about; indeed, the Punjaub was one of the brightest camps at the Durbar, and simply because of Major Dunlop Smith. One feels that one must talk about him. He is just the character of man we want in India—a man who is not only respected but also loved by the natives: a very strong character, yet intensely sympathetic. Major Dunlop Smith is destined to "go far." His grasp of detail is marvellous. I saw a good deal of his handling of the Chiefs' Retinue Procession, and it was simply wonderful. He was very thorough and complete, and set to work much as a painter would, keeping many of the groups straight with regard to placing in the procession. In short, he made them work from old pictures, pictures that he himself had brought from the Punjaub solely for that purpose.

One day, when we arrived at the Camp, the Major had around him two or three old native pictures, with a view to planning a portion of the Retainers' Procession on the same lines. He showed great appreciation, and when I examined these pictures I began to realise how excellent they were. I was in raptures. The technique was simply marvellous; the pigment pure and clear and crisp. These ancient Indian painters

A HINDOO HILL-SHEPHERD OF KASHMIR

The leather boots of this man are lined with fur, and he wears fur next to his skin, clothing which he found somewhat irksome during the fierce heat of Delhi.

had very different pigment from that which we use. It was curiously like the best of the old Chinese work; they must have used a very crisp white.

While I was explaining the beauties of one of these pictures to the Major, he suddenly talked of an artist, a native in whom he was very much interested, a man whom he would like me to meet. He sent for the artist. This was an opportunity I had longed for—to be able to talk technically to a native artist. In a way he expressed the feeling of Indian artists generally; and our conversation left me saddened rather and disappointed. I began by asking what white the old painters used. He said, "Oh, that white no good—only common white you buy in bazaars. Much better Chinese white—the white of Robertson you get in England—that very fine." I was disgusted. It was a knock-down blow to me; yet I battled with him. I got on to another track. I talked about the little clean-cut lines in some of the old work, lines no thicker than a hair, evidently put on with a brush so fine that one marvels how they could ever have been made. Here the artist was much more encouraging. He told me that for executing this fine work the brushes must be made specially by the artist. I was glad to hear him say this. He told me that all artists in India made their own brushes, especially those for doing the fine work, the small work.

A description of the native method of painting a picture, as nearly as possible as it was told to me by the artist, may be interesting. First of all you buy your black, in a sort of crystal; then you boil it and add a little gum. This is your black, the pigment used for outlining. Then you prepare your other colours in much the same way, by adding gum to the powders, and sometimes honey. In hot weather honey is always used, because it flows more freely. To test the proper consistency of the pigment, you put a little touch on your nail: if it should brush off it is evident that there is not enough honey. The natives do not use a muller, as we do, to grind colours: they use their thumb, and work the pigment round on a slab until it becomes an impalpable paste. When they have prepared their colours, they begin with a very fine brush to outline the subject in the finest possible lines with minute elaboration and completeness. Then they begin to mass in their broad tones, using body colour throughout. After these broad tones have been washed in, the picture

A SIKH WARRIOR

is by no means finished. It takes days to complete. They do not, as we do, load the colour and put it on thickly. They make infinite changes of colour in the washes, until they eventually get a solid patch of colour quite opaque. When the drawing is thus mapped out with these patches of opaque colour, they begin with very fine brushes to draw their detail. This they do in a series of hatching flat strokes from right to left, gradually using finer brushes as the space is filled up, and finish by little touches until the solid, compact, opaque tone has been procured. Then they begin to put in the finest detail of all, and by hatchings the shading becomes ever finer and finer until it looks as though it had been done in one wash. An artist will often finish up with a burnisher to get little microscopic touches, and, for very fine detail, so as to get a highly-finished surface. If in some of the pictures the artists have a good deal of gold, they use a chemical to change the colour of the gold to green-gold and red-gold, so as to make that particular portion harmonise with the rest of the picture.

Such, roughly, is the native method of painting a picture. "Of course you have learnt this method in the native schools?" I said.

"Oh no," he answered. "You can never learn these things in a native school: the artists will never tell one another anything: everything is a secret." I told him that, in my opinion, there should be no secrets in art. "Ah," he said, "in Europe it is different; but here everything is secret!"

I felt pleased with this artist, and satisfied. His description of the native method of painting had been very interesting, and had quite come up to my expectations. Directly afterwards he shattered all my hopes for Indian art in one fell swoop by remarking that this old method was of no use whatever, and that the only good principle was that of the Bombay School, which all the artists were now endeavouring to copy. After having listened to this fascinating description with enthusiasm, as though he knew what he was talking about and believed in it, to be told that he was following in the footsteps of the Bombay School of design was depressing. Then he went on to talk of perspective and drawing from the antique, and soon I began to feel that things were fairly hopeless. As a sort of final touch, he undid a paper parcel and showed me in a tawdry little gold frame an appalling miniature of the Viceroy

FROM THE HILLS, BALUCHISTAN

—niggled, small, and with no merit in it whatever. This man is a typical native artist. Nearly all his fellow-craftsmen seem to face art in the same way —so different from the artists in Japan, so much less artistic,—and we could not help feeling that there was in very truth no living art at all in India, and that the Viceroy, strive as hard as he may, will not produce revival.

After luncheon the Major took us to Jind, and there we saw a series of strange gentlemen. Sikhs they were, most of them dressed in blue, and bearing war implements and steel rings. They had circles of steel round their necks, similar circles round their turbans. At first it was a puzzle to me why they should carry these hoops; they were flat like quoits, had a sharp knife-edge, and appeared in most unexpected places—round the neck, round the waist, and on their turbans. Were they worn for decorative reasons? I discovered that the hoops were used simply as implements of war. They are deadly weapons. The Sikhs throw them at their enemies, hurl them along edgeways as you would a quoit, and cut off heads as easily as you would slice a lemon.

One of the incidents that attracted my attention

was the falsetto shriek of an old man standing under an archway at the entrance gate. He was a big man, though very old, with white hair and piercing black eyes; and he was mounted on a tiny pony, the size of a Shetland. He wore a huge conical turban, about four feet in height, covered with steel daggers, and hoops, and weapons of all kinds. He was a celebrated religious fanatic from the golden temple of Amritsar. The song he was singing was the names of ten Gurus in the form of a chant. A few days before the Sikhs had celebrated the birthday of Govind Sinh, the tenth and greatest Guru, the man who made the Sikhs into a religious and political power. The ninth Guru, Teg Bahadur, was a very religious man. His ambition was to reform the Sikhs; but he fell into the hands of the Great Mogul, who wanted to kill him, and was continually searching for some pretext to do so. At last Teg Bahadur, when walking outside his prison, was found guilty and accused of looking towards the Mogul's zenana, a heinous sin. He answered the accusation in these words: "I was not looking towards the zenana. I was looking south for the white race who will come from beyond the sea to tear down thy purdahs and destroy thine empire."

A TYPICAL BALUCH

He comes from the hills—a fierce, untamed creature.

Thus Teg Bahadur sealed his own fate. He was beheaded immediately. His words lived among the Sikhs afterwards, and his prophecy was spread far and wide; while his memory was kept green by the next Guru, the wise Govind Sinh. On the day when the Sikhs helped us so bravely at the assault of Delhi, and the Mogul rule was ended, Govind Sinh shouted out as a battle-cry the name of Teg Bahadur. That is partly the reason why the Sikhs are so friendly towards us. They feel that British rule in India has come to stay, and that it was the wish of Teg Bahadur, the great Guru, that it should be. The name of this great and glorious martyr acted as an impetus to their courage, and the Sikhs flung themselves boldly into the thick of the fight. The day of the Durbar the Sikhs made a pilgrimage to the tomb of Teg Bahadur to renew their vows of loyalty to the King Emperor. Their sacred book, the *Granth Sahib*, was brought forward, and they saluted it reverently while their bands played "God Save the King!" It was on this same anniversary that the screaming fanatic we saw at Jind clothed his pony in breeches and made a Sikh of him.

On another day, Major Dunlop Smith ordered

all the Baluchistan chiefs to be brought round to the Patiala Camp. There were about a hundred of them, all dressed in white—morose, severe-looking people. They were the very last to give in to British rule, and they didn't look as though they had quite given in yet, or as though they were likely to, so long as their race existed. They made a magnificent picture with their long jet-black beards, and their dark, extremely handsome faces. They wore long white flowing robes, and looked almost like biblical figures. I was surprised to find that etiquette was a great point with these men. They were extremely touchy, and stood on their dignity in quite a remarkable way. They would insist on being sketched each in his proper order. I chose one man to sit for me as being the most picturesque, and, to my astonishment, I found all the others turning their backs, and going off muttering, and glowering at me under their bushy eyebrows. However, they came back when I told them that they were necessary for my picture, and smiled and muttered among themselves, much like contented tiger-cats. These fierce hillmen are inordinately proud of their personal appearance.

When we left the Camp they came up to us

TWO BALUCH CHIEFS

WILD, untamed men, who seem as though they have not even yet completely subjected themselves to British rule.

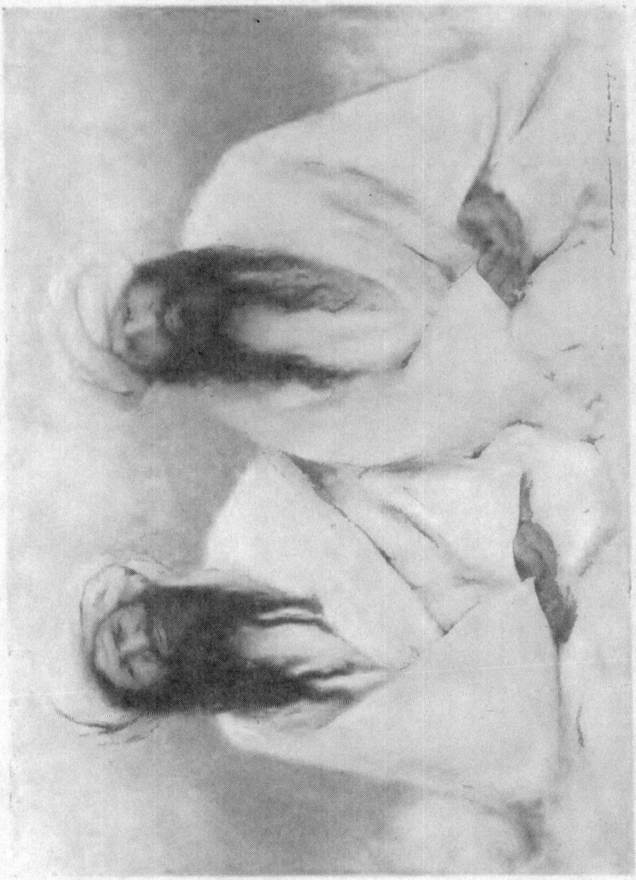

one at a time and insisted upon shaking hands. Most of them had never shaken hands in their lives before; but the first Chief, a more or less Europeanised person, had done it, and they must all follow suit. On one of the last days we spent at the Punjaub Camp, the Major told us of an interview he had with Nabha the old king. The Maharaja called on him, and said, "I shall soon be leaving Delhi now. I, the King, have rested on this ground in this Punjaub Camp; and I wish to place enough money in the bank to free this land from taxes for ever." As the Major said, this kingly speech was just like the dear old Nabha.

The Major was rather unhappy about the young Maharaja of Patiala. He was anxious, he said, to get the child away directly after the festivities. The boy's tendencies were somewhat frivolous, and he was enjoying the social side of the Durbar rather too heartily for the Major's peace of mind. The night before, he told us, Patiala had had an uproarious time at an evening party. The ladies had petted him, and he had become altogether too light-headed. It was time, said the Major, that the boy returned to his books. He was a kindly little chap, with a cheery nature, and with care, Dunlop Smith told us, he might develop into a very fine man; but he was so much surrounded by temptations, and his father's example had been so bad, that the Englishman's task was difficult.

THE MAHARAJA OF NABHA

One of the oldest Maharajas in Delhi. When leaving Delhi he placed sufficient money in the bank to free the land where his camp had been from taxes for ever. "For," he said, "I, the king, have rested here, and henceforth the land must always be free from encumbrances." A truly kingly act.

X

BARODA CAMP

SPEAR-BEARERS FROM CUTCH

A THRONG of mounted retainers, with silver-adorned saddlery.

X

BARODA CAMP

One day we went with the representative of *The Times* and other friends to lunch with the Gaekwar of Baroda. We were received by the Private Secretary, the Political Agent, and other officials, who took us into a large tent to sign our names in the visitors' book. It happened that just at that moment a neighbouring Maharaja had called on the Gaekwar. While waiting for our host, we looked at some of his jewels and the famous gold-and-silver cannons of Baroda. We were first taken to see the gold-and-silver ornaments of the oxen that drew the cannons. It was surprising to realise how many scores of thousands of pounds' worth of precious metal was kept in rickety old wooden boxes and guarded by an old man who seemed to be more or less of the coolie class. He had a bunch of clumsy keys, and it took him about half an hour before he could find the one to fit the lock of the box wherein these treasures lay. It did seem strange to see such priceless ornaments kept in so common a servant's bedroom chest of drawers; but thus it always is in India. One finds oneself surrounded by the most gorgeous splendour, and then suddenly comes across something paltry and incongruous.

We were taken to see the gold-and-silver cannons themselves,—the cannons that were to be paraded at the Durbar. There were only two of them. One was much older than the other. This one, built by a very distant ancestor, was a silver cannon supported on a brass stand. A more ambitious and more recent ancestor was determined to go farther. He therefore ordered a solid gold cannon to be constructed on a silver stand. There it was standing before us, blazing in the sun, so brilliant that it hurt one's eyes to look at it. The whole thing was all silver and gold—the wheels, the body of the carriage, and the ammunition holders all of silver; and the cannon itself, gold, solid gold. The Gaekwar has many more cannons; but these two were the only ones he brought to Delhi.

AN ELEPHANT FROM JAIPUR

In the end we saw so much gold that we began to talk of it by the pound weight. At every moment I held a handful of gold—now a jewelled garter worn by a sacred ox, and anon a solid gold covering for the horns, ten pounds in weight.

There was a surprise in store when we reached the tent where the Gaekwar's jewels were kept. They brought out a diamond necklace. It was almost a breastplate of diamonds of perfect purity—a necklace for which a millionaire might crave in vain. One diamond is said to be the third largest in the world, very little less than the "Koh-i-noor," the second largest. Hanging immediately underneath was a heart-shaped diamond, very nearly as large. Even these two massive gems did not appear so very enormous when surrounded, as they were, by scores of others, some of them larger than a child's marble. On seeing this wonder, a lady clasped her hands and exclaimed, "Oh why didn't His Highness wear that beautiful necklace at the Durbar?" "Because," said an official who was standing by, "that is only one among the Gaekwar's store of jewels. The necklace which His Highness wore at the Durbar was worth three times as much as this one. Here is something you will admire," he added, as he drew out a pearl necklace, five or six rows of pearls all as large as pigeon's eggs, so large that it seemed difficult to realise that they were in truth pearls. Through want of exposure to the light, they had become lustreless, and one felt that it would be good to throw them into the sea. There seemed to be over them a film which, if once unveiled, would reveal untold glories.

We went on from case to case seeing diamonds and rubies until our brains spun and we could see no more. The light and fire of those glorious gems were too much. It was a relief to leave them and go out into the open air again. The jewels fascinated one and exerted a strange influence.

The Gaekwar himself came forward to meet us as we entered the drawing-room. He was dressed in white satin edged with gold, and he wore five or six strings of pearls round his neck. He spoke in a most intelligent and interesting way. There can be no doubt that he is one of the most enlightened and powerful of Indian Princes. It seems strange that the Gaekwar was once only a village boy. In default of an heir, the Queen Dowager adopted and brought the child up as

WATCHING THE PAGEANT

successor to the vacant throne of Baroda. Also, it is strange that for all his ability, great wealth, and high position, this Prince is unable to persuade the poorest Brahmin begging at his gates to drink out of the same cup with him, or his high-caste neighbour to ally himself by marriage with his family.

The luncheon was modern and European, served on solid gold plate. The Political Resident was there—a man who is supposed to counteract the Ruler's conduct in affairs of State—to humour him and yet stand firm. That is a somewhat difficult position ordinarily; but with the Gaekwar of Baroda the Resident's post is quite a sinecure. The State is so sensibly governed that the Resident has developed into a companion to the Gaekwar when he travels, and his chief duty consists in insisting that proper respect is paid to his Highness's person.

The ladies of our party went into the zenana, and were entertained by the Maharani of Baroda. They told me their experiences afterwards, and were one and all enthusiastic in praise of their hostess. She talked and gossiped with them, they said, like any English lady. Indeed, she is an enlightened Princess. She has been to London with her husband, and has mixed in English society. She is never seen by any man save her husband, not even by the British Resident; and she affirms that "native public opinion is not yet prepared for any radical change in the condition of Indian women." She took the ladies into her bedroom, they told me; and her maid brought out all her dresses—cases and cases of them—cloth of gold, silks sewn with pearls and rubies and diamonds, silver-spangled chiffons, and endless joys such as made them terribly envious.

XI

THE SIKKIM CAMP

CHIEFS OF THE SHAN STATE

XI

THE SIKKIM CAMP

EVERYTHING was native in the Sikkim Camp. There was less money spent on it than on any other at the Durbar. Still, perhaps just because there was no attempt at the introduction of European furniture, the effect was quite splendid. Directly one passed the threshold one felt in another world. These people were more gentle, more easy to understand, more emotional, than the Indians. They seemed to be more of the temperament of the Burmese, and showed their feelings more. I noticed an old man sitting down on a stone, crying. He stayed there for some time in the same position, always weeping. When I asked them why he was showing this extreme grief, they told me that he had had his money stolen from him that morning, and he had been crying ever since. There he was, when I left, still sobbing just like a baby.

I was told that the young ruler of Sikkim had helped to design and to carry out much of the decoration of the Camp himself. This was in order to economise; for Sikkim is not a rich State, and he was so anxious to make a good show. Where riches failed taste stepped in, and in my opinion at least far eclipsed the other. The whole Camp was very artistic in the way it had been planned out. Unfortunately, it was so far away that very few people went to see it. Of the large tents, one was used for a reception-room, and full of interest, almost like a museum, filled as it was with quaint curios very well placed, arousing more interest than the art exhibition. The camp costume was different from any other I had seen. There was not all that gold and gorgeousness: it was very simple, and the colours were subdued. In fact, the people in appearance reminded me of the Burmese. There was a girl there who acted as a servant to one of the ladies, and she was quite pretty and fascinating. Indeed, what struck me most forcibly about the Sikkim Camp was the simplicity of the people. They were like a camp of children.

After leaving the Sikkim Camp we went over to the Burmese. There we saw the famous gong

A SOLDIER OF THE MAHARAJA OF SIKKIM

THIS is the old dress of the men in the Raja's army; they are especially proud of the peacock's feathers in their caps.

which is carried in all religious ceremonies and great processions. The men who bore it wore enormous hats — Leghorn hats — very much like those worn by London omnibus-horses in summer. This Burmese Camp was quite distinct. Here one met with perfect joy. It was all happiness, and the people showed their joy in every way; yet it was not an energetic, it was a languid, happiness. We were entertained there by one of the Shan Chiefs, and presented to his wife and family with much ceremony. When we arrived they were all smoking enormous cheroots—the wife, the servants, and even the pretty children—and cigars which were quite a foot in length. I never saw people who were slower or more dignified. We were presented to them by an official, and quite five minutes passed before anything was said to us at all. The Chief went on smoking and drinking small cups of strong tea, and so did the family. Then the lord and master spoke, but only for a few seconds: he went on again smoking and sipping his tea. It was quite ten minutes before we were made known to the wife and family. These last were more or less subservient: they all seemed to be occupied in looking after the Chief—his tea, and the lighting of his cigar. They all sat for me just in front of the tent, surrounded by their paraphernalia for tea-drinking and smoking.

The women were exceedingly pretty; their hair was dressed very smartly, as neatly coifed, indeed, as that of American women: it was carefully brushed until it was glossy. Their faces were whitened and their lips painted a brilliant carmine. They all wore a flower, generally a pink one, in their hair. Each costume composed a different scheme of colour. They all wore silks, and the wife had a soft, rose-coloured skirt, with a little white cambric bodice and black satin band round her waist. She was quite a poem! Throughout the whole Camp I noticed that the colouring was fair and delicate—not the rich vermilions and reds of India, but delicate rose tones, pinks, and blues. This was the colouring that met one's eyes everywhere in the Burmese Camp. It was a gracious relief.

A SHAN CHIEF AND HIS WIFE

He drinks tea and smokes cheroots all day long, while it is her duty to talk to him and amuse him.

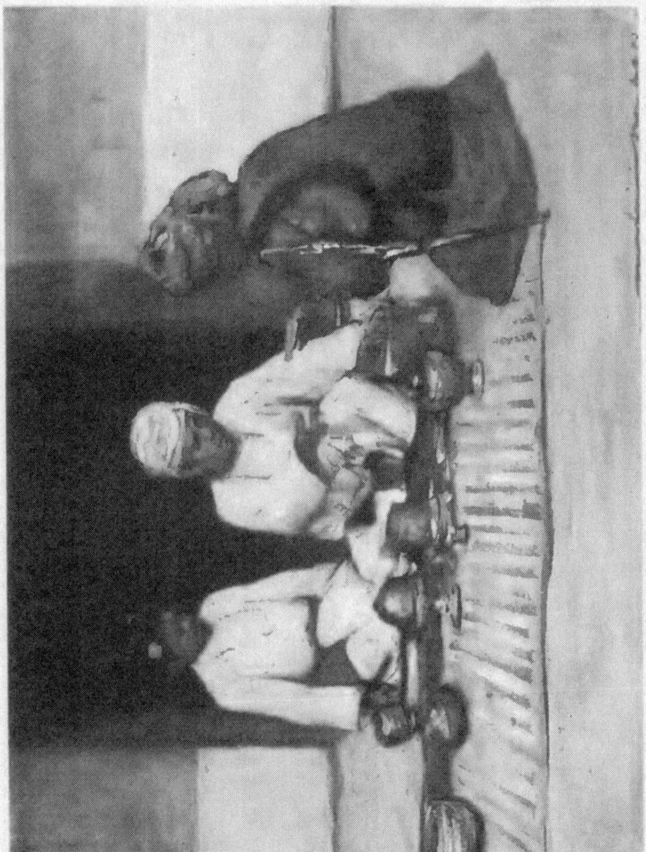

XII

THE CENTRAL INDIA CAMP

A HAWKSMAN OF RAJGARH

XII

THE CENTRAL INDIA CAMP

We started for the Central India Camp very early in the morning; but, as usual, we lost our way, and did not arrive until late. The British Resident in charge was not quite so charming as most of the men with whom we had come in contact. Perhaps we had been spoiled by the extreme courtesy we had met with everywhere in India. All the camps were rather near, and we walked from one to the other.

In Dhar there were some particularly magnificent elephants, with silver howdahs and gold saddle-cloths, driven by men in purple-and-gold with gold-and-orange turbans. The retainers were in brown with red turbans. Then, there was a real old warrior, with a gold helmet, carrying an orange banner—an old man standing apart in the sun in a yellow jacket, blue breastplate, orange-

and-gold waistband, and turban of the same hue, in his hand a lance with red streamers.

At Narsinghgarh there was a huge elephant with a boy sitting astride its tusks; high above him towered a great golden howdah and a small golden umbrella; hanging about him were red velvet and golden tassels.

Every one was only too anxious to sit to me at Rajgarh. Some arranged themselves against a tawdry temporary erection, and tried to elbow one another out in order to get good positions. I moved them all about as I chose, pushing some back and pulling others forward. I found out afterwards that these were all great men, and that I had been pushing about Commanders-in-Chief and Rajas. They all wore differently-coloured dresses. There were two venerable men with very white beards in light blue with orange turbans and pink sashes. Others were in black with coloured pompons. Some had old-rose and silver dresses; others sported butter colour with pink turbans. All carried flaming banners. It was superb—a marvellous collection. There were the dogs and the falconers—a magnificent group. One of the falconers carried a bird on his gloved hand. He was dressed in vivid colours, and was a

A STANDARD-BEARER OF CUTCH

PERHAPS one of the finest figures at the Durbar.

splendid type. Then, the hounds, a whole pack of them, had bright yellow jackets edged with red and brilliant grass-green; so on, and so on. They seemed to be building up in beauty of colouring, these camps of the native Chiefs: each seemed more brilliant than the last. The officer who was looking after us seemed much more interested in a motor car than in native costume or art; but even his lack of enthusiasm could not damp us. Everything we saw was a picture, and the people themselves were intensely interested.

Perhaps one of the finest figures I saw in India was in Central India. He was a standard-bearer, with a gold helmet and steel chain-armour. It was the dignity of the man that impressed me chiefly. He had a black beard parted at his chin and brushed smartly up to his ears. He carried an enormous orange banner with a gold device, and his horse wore trappings of blue with a red and green checked saddle-cloth. This figure we saw later at the Retainers' show. He stood out even surrounded by so much fine manhood.

Scindia had only begun to prepare when we arrived. We could not wait for him, and went on to Rewa. Rewa was especially gorgeous. There we saw vivid emerald-green banners and elephants with gold trappings. To describe in detail the costumes and trappings of the various animals would be wearisome, and would not convey a true impression. You can only imagine all the most brilliant colours you have ever seen, and then understand that these were twice as brilliant and in motion in a clear atmosphere under a burning sun—colours that you could not look at in any country save India, for they would blind you. Rewa seemed to be the last word in gorgeousness. One had seen elephants smothered in gold, and horses caparisoned in vivid colours; but here they had gone as far as they could go in gorgeous colour and richness of detail. For example, there would be an elephant with the driver and the bearers all in gold, and in different qualities of gold—all gold. My poor little palette compared with this sparkle in sunlight was almost pathetic.

In Gwalior we noticed a levelling influence, a change. The colour was sadder, and the costume fast disappearing, giving place to Western improvements and military ideas. It made one reflect, and was depressing for the moment.

This wonderful Central India Camp, with all its priceless gems and glittering heaps of precious

A FORMIDABLE WARRIOR OF REWA

THE spiky armour of this old gentleman rattled, as he walked, like a lot of kitchen utensils.

metals, obliged one to realise how extremely lucky it was to have seen the Durbar. Strangers passing through India visit the different show-places; they "do" the temples and the ruins; and sometimes, through special letters of introduction, they call on the various Rajas. But they never see the marvellous stores of gold and jewels hidden away in the inner apartments of the Palaces, or, if they do, it is among more or less tawdry surroundings. To the Durbar every Raja brought his best and costliest; each vied with his neighbour in pride of possession; and we saw all these treasures massed together in one glittering heap against a dignified and suitable background.

OF THE IMPERIAL CADET CORPS

One of the gallant members of a corps which is considered the finest in India—a slim young prince whose very bearing suggests noble birth.

XIII

THE BOMBAY AND IMPERIAL CADET CORPS

XIII

THE BOMBAY AND IMPERIAL CADET CORPS

SOME of the handsomest and most distinguished types we saw in India were at the Bombay Camp. The difficulty was to make selections for pictures: they were all characteristic and splendid.

Some of the Bombay Chiefs refused to live in the tents allotted to them, and took houses in the village near by. Most of the camps were very elaborately prepared, neat and smart. For example, one never saw waste-paper lying about at the Bombay Camp. There were picturesque archways, gravelled paths, splendid drainage, large reception tents, and some had stained-glass windows. Some had gardens. All were illuminated by electric light. Cutch was proud in the possession of a camp made entirely of velvet with poles of silver; it was like one great and perfect Eastern carpet, such as one sometimes sees in some Bond Street shop. One of the Chiefs of Bombay had a curious fancy. He lived in a quiet little house just out of the bazaar with an old-world garden, far from the haunts of men. A very good idea, too, I thought; far more attractive in some ways than many of the gaudier dwelling-places of brother Chiefs.

On the way home from the Bombay Chiefs' Camp we called at the Camp of the Imperial Cadet Corps. We were met by Major Thompson, a very alert man. He immediately took us round the camp and explained everything—the reason for the formation of the corps, its results, its dangers, the life of the boys indoors and out. He himself taught them lessons in English and arithmetic. We were taken to the stables and shown the famous horses, beautiful black creatures wearing red coverings to keep the dust off, for, as Major Thompson said, they become brown and rusty soon if they have not constant attention. He introduced us to H.H. the Maharaja of Idar, Honorary Colonel of the Imperial Cadet Corps, popularly known as Sir Pratap Singh.

HORSEMAN AT THE BOMBAY CAMP

ONE of the handsomest and most daring riders at the Durbar.

His Royal Highness, without a collar on, was sitting on his bed, looking happy and buoyant, brimming over with high spirits. He seemed on very friendly terms with all the men, who treated him as if he were a brother. I stayed there for over half an hour, and we had a long conversation—Major Thompson, Sir Pratap Singh, and myself. I was much impressed with the keen way in which they both talked. They were both full of enthusiasm and eagerly discussed the uniform of the Cadets. Sir Pratap Singh wondered if it was perhaps too pretty: he thought that perhaps it wanted relieving somewhere with a touch of blood-red. The two officers had worked out the scheme of the uniform themselves. We had a long and interesting talk about the corps. Sir Pratap Singh said that it was, of course, quite an experiment. He didn't know exactly how it would end; but his object was to make men of the Cadets, and to show them that there were other things to do in this world than merely luxuriating and leading a dissolute life—for men in their position there was a real and good work at hand. They seemed to think that it was an interesting experiment, and hoped that in the end it would be a gigantic success.

It was Sir Walter Lawrence's idea that we should visit the camp and sketch the Cadets. The Cadet Corps was a pet scheme of his. In fact, it was he and the Viceroy who originated it.

BOMBAY CHIEFS' CAMP

THE golden ornaments on the top of their banners are emblems which have been bestowed upon them by the Mogul Emperors. In one of the golden balls is some sacred water from the Ganges, which, if sprinkled on a dying man during battle, will ensure his entrance into heaven.

XIV

THE VICEROY

ARMOURED HORSEMEN OF KISHENGARH

THESE men with their coats of chain armour and metal helmets remind one of the warriors of the Middle Ages, and strike far greater terror into the hearts of their enemies than would our modern khaki soldiers.

XIV

THE VICEROY

Towards the end of the Durbar, at a time when one was fully able to appreciate the power of Lord Curzon, I found myself, paint-box in hand and trepidation in my heart, waiting an audience with the great man. I had had many chances of studying him before, at dinner, driving in the streets, and at different ceremonies; but this was to be the final sitting.

I had been shown into an ante-room by an A.D.C., and had sat down to wait. A few minutes later the door opened and Mr. E. T. Reed made his appearance. "Hullo! what are you doing here?" I asked. "I am going to paint the Viceroy," he answered. "Impossible!" I cried. "Why, I am here for the same purpose!" "Then, we shall have to paint him together," we murmured as with one voice, collapsing. We sat down uncomfortably on the edges of chairs, and had a furtive talk. There was a chilly, nervous atmosphere about that room. Neither of us is timid by nature; yet we felt its influence. Cold shivers stole down our backs and depression settled on our spirits. We talked to one another in whispers. Reed said it reminded him of a dentist's waiting-room. I have never been in one, but could sympathise. We had always helped each other, Reed and I, from the first start off on the boat; and even here we feebly tried to buck each other up. "Look here, Menpes," said Reed: "you ought to be all right: you sketched Lord Kitchener the other day, and that must have been a splendid rehearsal." I admitted that it certainly should have been, but said that I did not feel fortified. "Now, you, Reed," I added encouragingly, "you're different: you've got such habits—you have painted the Duke of Connaught." He murmured something about not feeling stimulated, and reminded me of my portrait of the Duke of Hesse. Both were floored in a vain attempt to be cheerful, and studied the pattern of the carpet for some minutes in silence. Suddenly Reed and I looked up, and the only picture in the room caught our attention at the same moment. It was the typical

LADY CURZON

A LADY whose popularity is only excelled by her beauty.

amateurish picture with very brilliant colouring, juicy pigment, and the usual figure in a red shawl that most beginners seem to think it necessary to introduce into their landscapes. Reed and I were enthusiastic. We peered into the picture, examined it from all angles, talked of its technique, until the landscape assumed the proportions of a masterpiece. The artist, we declared, must be a genius. Reed said he liked the nice crisp drawing; I said it was a gorgeous bit of colour.

In the midst of our feverish criticism, and as though to save us from dotage, Lady Curzon swept into the room, a vision of beauty in the palest of lilac gowns. She carried me off to the drawing-room, and by her ready tact and sympathy soon dispelled my nervousness and made the way smooth. What an ideal wife for a Viceroy, I thought! She was looking extremely well, not in the least fatigued; and when I asked her if she did not feel the effects of the Durbar she said that work was meat and drink to her.

Soon an A.D.C. entered to usher me into the presence of the Viceroy. I was shown into a room that was being used as a study. Lord Curzon was at his desk, writing. The moment I was announced he sprang up. His movements were very active. Holding out his hand to me, he said, "So I hear you want to paint me, Mr. Menpes?" I said I was very anxious to do so. He looked quickly round the room, his keen eyes taking in everything, and said, "Now, what about the light? Do you think the light is good, or do you think it would be better on the verandah? Perhaps it would be as well if you surveyed a little first, and then told me where to sit. I shall be prepared at any moment." I liked this. There was no waste of time, yet no nervous hurry: he took in the situation at a glance with a tactfulness that charmed me.

I went round with the A.D.C. and chose a position in the verandah.

Without any delay the Viceroy came and sat. He was wearing a gray frock-coat, and had a flower in his button-hole. He looked crisp and well-groomed, and in the keen, searching light one had a splendid chance of studying his expressions, which were changing constantly. What an alert face! With what bright, clear eyes he met my glance! Assurance seemed stamped in every line of those strong, almost stern, features. One felt that to this man there was no such thing as the insurmountable. In proportion to the

A RAJPUT OF RAJGARH

face Lord Curzon's head is enormous. It is an obviously intelligent head; at the back it seems to have burst out into bulges with intelligence. I was struck not only by the strength and intelligence of the man before me, but also by his kindliness and sympathy. Whatever Lord Curzon's critics may say, after that one sitting in his verandah at Delhi, I shall always maintain that the Viceroy of India is a magnetic man, a sympathetic man, a stimulating man, a man who has the power to draw the very best out of people. To me as a painter he showed the most delightful side of his character. Busy beyond words, he allowed himself to drift sympathetically, giving me the impression that time was of no consequence, and art the only thing to live for. He did not sit down with watch in hand and say, "Now paint me," as I have known lesser men do. He talked just as an artist would talk. He stimulated me, and got me in the right condition for work: in a word, he made me feel restful, which is the proper mood for a painter.

"Well, and how did the Durbar appeal to you from the painter's standpoint?" he asked. I told him that it had appealed to me because of its completeness. I had admired the arrangement of the colour-schemes and the knowledge and artistic feeling shown even in the erection of the temporary buildings. Above all, I had been struck by the oneness of it—by its being the work of one man. In fact, if I remember right, I think I called the Durbar a "one-man's show."

Lord Curzon's face lit up as I spoke, and he smiled at me radiantly, for he is fond of his work, and he felt that he had achieved a triumph. "Ah," he said, "but you must not forget, Mr. Menpes, that I have been surrounded by splendid lieutenants, splendid workers who have carried out my intentions to the minutest detail!" Despite that, a few words with the great man was enough to convince me that the Durbar had been created solely by himself.

Lord Curzon talked of the art of the country and of the bad influence that had been brought to bear on it. One felt that he had really studied this subject, and that it came very near to him. He realised as no one else seemed to have done that the art of India was slipping away, and that if vigorous measures were not taken to foster and encourage it we should live to say that there was no living art in India. He touched a little, but very lightly, on the subject of the Exhibition that had

AN ARMED RETAINER OF THE BOMBAY CHIEFS

He is a great person in his State; at his back he carries a shield made of polished hippopotamus hide.

been opened at Delhi. The word *bazaar* was on the tip of my tongue. Personally, I thought it was the most hopeless show I had ever seen, involved and foolish; and I could not help understanding by the tone of Lord Curzon's voice that he, too, felt full well that the Exhibition was anything but successful in placing and arrangement.

"I fear your first two days in camp were not altogether satisfactory in relation to your work, Mr. Menpes," said Lord Curzon suddenly, after a pause, during which I had been feverishly trying to seize a certain dreamy expression often seen on his face. I was amazed at the question. Then, he knew? He had read my letter to the Military Secretary asking to be transferred from the Millionaires' Camp to the Press Camp! The Viceroy went on: "We were uncertain where to place you. Here, in my Camp, you would have been distracted from your work, and we were not sure if you cared to be in the Press Camp; so temporarily you were placed in Number One Camp. When you wrote to my Military Secretary expressing a wish to be transferred, it was immediately done; and I hope you are thoroughly satisfied." No man could have said more; it was just the right thing to stimulate me; it showed tact, intuition, and knowledge of "the artistic temperament." How thorough the man is! Nothing escapes him. I was only one of thousands; yet he knew everything about me, and showed a keen interest in my affairs. "I know your work well, Mr. Menpes," he said, with a smile as he noticed my look of astonishment. "You have come here to do a big work; but no one is better equipped for the task of depicting these great ceremonies than yourself, absorbed as you are with the gorgeous colouring of the East." This is an instance of Lord Curzon's marvellous memory, and I dare guarantee that every man who came in contact with him in Delhi would have similar stories to relate.

When the sitting was over and I had completed my work, Lord Curzon chose exactly the right moment to dismiss me; and he did it in a graceful way. He hoped I would come to Calcutta, and described several scenes that I certainly must portray in different parts of India. I said that Delhi had absorbed me—that I wished to see nothing more. I wanted to work hard at my exhibition of the Durbar pictures, and keep away from other impressions until they were finished. Every moment during the Durbar was precious; but the instant it was over I intended to fly away

CAMELS FROM MYSORE

on a P. and O. boat and work, for I wanted to be alone. Lord Curzon turned to me, with a smile and a bow, and said, "If every moment is precious and you want to be alone, you must not linger here with me—I had better go!" With these graceful words my never-to-be-forgotten talk with the Viceroy of India ended.

As I passed through the ante-room on my way out, I cast an eye at the picture that Reed and I had so much admired. Pleased and elated with the success of my sitting, and with Lord Curzon's stimulating individuality, I looked at it with other eyes. The picture appeared in its true light: it was crude and poor and weak. Where was the gorgeous colouring? I looked about for Reed; but he had disappeared.

XV

LORD KITCHENER

LORD KITCHENER

THE Commander-in-Chief's Camp during the Durbar was one of the gayest and most brilliant in Delhi; he himself was genuinely sorry when the party had to be broken up at the end of the fortnight.

XV

LORD KITCHENER

Everyone helped me to persuade Lord Kitchener to sit—Colonel Rhodes, Colonel Hamilton, and others. They had all talked to the Chief about sitting, and he had promised each one faithfully that he would. It was some time before I heard from any of them; but at length I received an urgent letter from Colonel Hamilton saying that Lord Kitchener would be ready to sit to me the next morning at nine. Somehow, I rather feared this sitting. I felt that, being so much occupied and in such a hurry, Lord Kitchener would be brusque and unsympathetic.

We were determined to be before rather than after the stated time, and in our anxiety arrived at the Commander-in-Chief's Camp at a quarter to nine. A bit ashamed, we wandered about in our little tonga, and were just in time to see Lord

Kitchener return from his morning ride. At nine o'clock to the minute we were shown into the reception-room. Shortly afterwards Colonel Hamilton joined us there, and took us into an inner room—Lord Kitchener's study. It was a large tent, and rather dark. The Commander-in-Chief was sitting at his desk, writing. He was exceedingly kind and sympathetic, took a real interest in my work, and was not nearly so difficult a sitter as I had expected him to be. At the same time, he struck me as being intensely shy—not at all the same man I remembered on the kopje at Osfontein in the midst of battle. Even the character of his face seemed to have changed. He was a different person. There was a softening, a distinct alteration. The whole time I was painting him I noticed that he seemed self-conscious. I was aware that he longed for the sitting to be over, not so much because he disliked it as because he was really shy. Still, he was jovial withal, entirely sympathetic and kindly. He looked serious during the sitting, almost tragic; but it seemed a passing expression on a jovial face. As we entered he stood up, and Colonel Hamilton introduced us to him. Then there was a pause, and nothing was said for a moment, until I

SPEAR-BEARER FROM JIND

The steel circles in his turban are not only for decoration, but for use in warfare.

mumbled out an apology for asking him to sit. He said at once, "I think this room is too dark. I don't believe you will be able to see me; but you can try." With that he sat down and stared straight at me, as rigid as a sphinx; and so long as I painted him he fixed me with those brilliant steel-blue eyes of his. It was a little unnerving at first. After a time he shook off his shyness, and began to talk about the Durbar and the possibilities for my work, expressing his opinion that in the native Chiefs' camps I should secure my best material. By the time I had sketched him in the tent I became bolder, and begged that he would sit outside. This was rather daring, for there he would be seen by other people, and in answer, Lord Kitchener murmured something I did not quite hear, which showed me clearly that it was not altogether his pleasure. Still, so many friends of mine had talked to him about this sitting that he felt that he must go through with it. He braced himself together manfully and came out. He sat outside in the sun in a rigid and dogged way, and the moment I said that I had finished he sprang up and rushed into his tent. We followed; and he stood up and talked, but not for long, and we left hurriedly.

Directly we came out of Lord Kitchener's tent

we were besieged by a group of his guests, all eager to know how we had found the "Chief,"—how he had looked, and what he had said. They were all full of stories about him, and were delighted with their stay in his Camp. He was a perfect host, they said, always jovial and good-tempered.

The Commander-in-Chief's Camp was certainly the brightest and gayest and happiest in the whole Durbar, not in the least what one would have expected it to be. He was always anxious for his friends' comfort, they said. One day, I was told, he took some of them out to a picnic, and spent the whole day with them. Strange to say, he seemed to delight in ladies' society: one lady told me that on the last day, when they were all breaking up, he was really grieved to say good-bye to them. The reports stating Lord Kitchener is a woman-hater are, I should say, quite false. His aversion from ostentation and display, however, is not at all overrated. Lord Kitchener hates what he terms "unnecessary fuss." One day one of his young officers drew his attention to a fine body of men who were waiting outside the tent: they were to form his escort at some important Durbar ceremony. Lord Kitchener immediately flew into a towering rage, and exclaimed that he would not

FROM RAJGARH

have all those men following him about. It was not until the officer had timidly explained how hurt the men would be if they were not allowed to escort him that he grudgingly assented. Then, again, his dislike to publicity was shown at Simla. There every one expected that he would take a large house and entertain lavishly; but after he had been over to choose the ground, they found to their great chagrin that he had selected a very small place far from the madding crowd.

BALUCH CHIEFS ON DURBAR DAY

CROSSING the plain on the way to their seats in the grand amphitheatre.

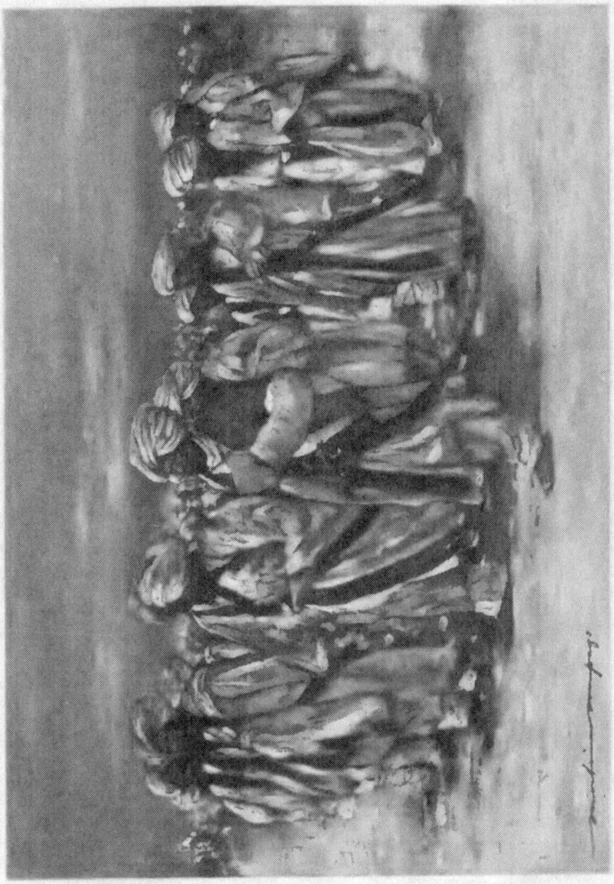

XVI

REFLECTIONS

AN ELEPHANT OF CENTRAL INDIA

One of the fifteen massive elephants from Gwalior.

XVI

REFLECTIONS

WHEN one reflects upon the Durbar as a whole, and thinks of its effect upon native and European alike all over India, one cannot but worship and bow down to that marvellous brain at the back of all, the man who pulled the strings—Lord Curzon. The politician of the village pump declaimed against the Durbar. It was a waste of money, he said—a useless display of splendour. Let us argue with him, then: let us proceed to justify the Durbar.

To begin with, the home-staying wiseacre does not realise that for centuries the Oriental idea of power has been connected with superb shows and ceremonies, and that the natives would regard anything done in a plain way as poor, and look down, not so much upon the show itself as upon the British Empire which had produced it. The very fact that in a moment of time a Western

Ruler should come and beat them on their own ground has established in the mind of prince and peasant alike a lasting impression of the position of the British Raj which nothing else could possibly have achieved. Then, again, that Lord Curzon was able to bring together under one roof for the first time one hundred independent Chiefs and Rulers from all over India, many of them never having seen one another before, was in itself a great *tour de force.* Think what a tremendous lesson the Durbar must have been to these men! Whatever expense we may have been put to, that alone is a justification. It not only made the natives realise the great power of the British Empire, but also fired them with loyalty and caused them to be knit together in bonds of fealty.

The Durbar acted on a concentration of loyalty which spread itself all over India. To many of the great Rulers the British Empire must have been something misty and intangible; but all the mystery and intangibility passed away, as it were, and was translated to the clear and concrete, when they stood in the presence of the Empire's Viceroy and in the presence of the brother of the Emperor himself. They realised then that, great as they themselves were, and great as their fathers had

A SLIPPER-MAKER

been before them, eminently greater was the Ruler of England and the Indies and much else of the world besides. At the Military Review, these Princes were able to see a force of 30,000 men. Those among them who thought at all must have said to themselves, "Look at that! How splendid! Who has done it all?" The answer must have instantly suggested itself: "It has all been done by the Emperor!" They realised the power of the Sovereign they have over them, and went home with new ideas of discipline, saturated with pride and loyalty; and they spread these feelings far and wide throughout their States.

The Durbar contained a lesson not only for the Indian people, but also for the whole world,—one which the whole world would do well to lay to heart. Gathered there together under the roof of that great amphitheatre were the representatives of one half of the whole human race. There were the old Powers of Europe; the young republic in America; the countries of the Far East, such as China and Japan—all of these must have realised, as perhaps they never did before, how vast is this great Empire and its influence how far-reaching.

Lord Curzon is possessed of all the qualities that are necessary to a successful Viceroy—energy, eloquence, immense persuasive powers and vigour, a habit of refusing to recognise anything as insurmountable, and a perfect disbelief that any one is better than himself. He made his power felt in every detail of the Durbar. Everything you saw you knew that Lord Curzon had done. Nothing was too big or too small for his consideration, and his grasp of detail was just as strong as his breadth of understanding. He neglected nothing, from the large temporary buildings to the placing of a little elastic band on the official directory.

From an artistic point of view the Durbar was irreproachable. The handling of the elephants as a mass, the colour-scheme, the construction of the temporary buildings—everything was carried out in an artistic way. No painter could have complained of the Durbar. I myself criticised it from that standpoint, and was astonished. Even Rembrandt could not have handled the affair better.

When Lord Curzon first went out to India he went there full of vigour and energy. One of the first things he did was to reform official documents, the wordy documents which took one so long to read. He was determined to master detail, and it was impossible to do so

A STATE ELEPHANT IN ALL ITS TRAPPINGS

Even among such a gorgeous display as the native review this elephant attracted attention.

unless things were presented to him in simple and clear forms. The reform of these official documents was a big task; but he did not shirk it, and at length the herculean labour was completed. As things are now, with a few crisp sentences one can take in a situation at a glance, instead of wading through many pages of foolscap. After simplifying the official documents Lord Curzon started his wider reforms. That superb machine, composed of permanent officials, our great staff in India, up till then had been a little apathetic, rather stagnant. The Viceroy began to move it. Some people said he did so too rapidly; but Lord Curzon knew better. Any movement at all would have been resented by a machine which had settled down as this one had. One might liken it to a ship anchored on a rock in still water and suddenly boarded by an energetic commander who meant to move. Every one aboard was sick. Even the officers were sick. They were not used to such movement. It was comparatively gentle in itself; but by contrast to the former stillness it appeared violent.

This action of Lord Curzon in India was absolutely necessary. Only a bold man could have attempted such a tremendous work. Only a bold reformer, and no one who has not visited India, can comprehend the magnitude of it. For example, Lord Curzon attacked the Caste Question. Englishmen in India have supremacy over the natives, and Englishmen have abused it. The Viceroy announced in his speeches that equal justice must be meted out to native and to European. Up to a very recent period, before Lord Curzon came to India, it was almost impossible to obtain capital punishment for a white soldier who had murdered a native. I know perfectly well that the theory of Empire is based on the supremacy of the white man over the black; but there is a right and a wrong way of demonstrating this supremacy, and in the past the wrong way predominated.

Here are two instances which actually occurred not long ago in the Bombay presidency. One day a subaltern got into a first-class railway carriage and found sitting there a "coloured gentleman." In a fit of rage, he seized the poor man by the shoulders, and, shouting out to him, "Out you go, you black beast!" pitched him and his portmanteaus on to the platform. This, to his great astonishment, caused a considerable disturbance; and when he inquired what the people meant by putting themselves out over a black man, an Englishman who was passing by answered: "Well, perhaps you don't know it, but you have just thrown one of Her Majesty's judges out of the train." On another occasion Lord R——, a great governor, had a big dinner-party, at which were present a certain Anglo-Indian official of some importance and his wife. Lord R——, with a "coloured gentleman" at his side, walked up to the lady and said, "Will you allow me to introduce my friend Mr. S——? He will take you into dinner." She, without taking the slightest notice of the "coloured gentleman," threw up her head, walked up to her husband, and the two marched out of the room together. The whole of Anglo-India was on her side! It is easy to understand, then, the vast importance and magnitude of the task that Lord Curzon set himself to do. He set his face as a flint against the many outrages which were being perpetrated by Anglo-Indians against native Indians. It required much courage; but he carried on his crusade logically. It did not help to make him popular with the military out there; and, as these are the people who surround him socially, whom he must live with day after day, it is obvious that only a courageous and strong man could have pursued this course.

Then, he says that if we are to retain India we must respect the native prejudices and traditions, religious, social, and other. With a view to carrying this out, he has turned his attention to the shooting. Certain birds, such as the peacock, are sacred; but Tommy went out shooting peacocks galore. Now Lord Curzon has laid down strict and stringent laws. Soldiers must not go out shooting unless they are able to speak the language, which practically means that Tommy cannot shoot at all. This doesn't exactly help to make Lord Curzon popular with the army; but, after all, was ever a great reformer universally popular?

THE END